An Oxford graduate, Jerry Rhodes began h[...]
ter, making a life-changing switch in his [...]
management, first in Hoover and then in [...] up
Training in Rank Xerox UK before promotion to Rank Organization Personnel brought experience of corporate politics. An
invitation from Kepner Tregoe to become UK Managing Director
gave new openings on the international front and in 1975 led to his
establishing his own consultancy, Joint Development Resources,
specializing in creativity.

On completing her degree at Leeds University, Sue Thame started
out in journalism, then moved into staff and management training
in Fleet Street. A spell with the Manpower Services Commission
convinced her of her own need to delve more deeply into the
mysteries of learning and development. She studied full time for
three years, becoming a teacher of the Alexander technique and
building her own freelance work. Co-founding and directing an
Alexander Centre from 1979–85 led to many requests to help
people manage stress and awaken creativity.

JOINT DEVELOPMENT RESOURCES

Joint Development Resources was founded by Jerry Rhodes in
1975 as a consultancy to encourage creativity in business. Our field
is know-how in generic thinking skills. We specialize in the kind of
research that penetrates into management competencies, and we
have developed the 'human software', in the form of printed and
taped materials, to make these core skills tangible and within the
grasp of everyone.

A hallmark of our approach is 'joint development' with colleagues and clients. Our training packages provide bespoke mental
toolkits for ongoing learning, since both people and organizations
must continuously learn if they are to survive and succeed. We seek
to inspire the learning organizations of the future which will ensure
that systems and structures support and complement the creative,
caring and innovative thinking of their members.

Joint Development Resources is based at [...]
Middlesex, HA5 5HH, tel. no. (01) 866 126[...]

Jerry Rhodes and Sue Thame
Cotswold House
16 Bradley Street
Wotton-under-Edge
Gloucestershire GL12 7AR
Tel (01453) 521585 Fax 521686

Jerry Rhodes and Sue Thame

THE COLOURS
OF YOUR MIND

FONTANA/Collins

First published in 1988 by Collins
8 Grafton Street, London W1X 3LA
First issued in Fontana paperbacks in 1989

Copyright © Jerry Rhodes and Sue Thame 1988

Printed and bound in Great Britain by
William Collins Sons & Co. Ltd, Glasgow

CONDITIONS OF SALE

This book is sold subject to the condition that
it shall not, by way of trade or otherwise, be
lent, re-sold, hired out or otherwise circulated
without the publisher's prior consent in any
form of binding or cover other than that
in which it is published and without a similar
condition including this condition being
imposed on the subsequent purchaser.

Contents

'An entirely new approach to thinking – important reading for anyone involved in running meetings, team building, project management or decision-making . . . Groups using the processes described will undoubtedly benefit by increasing mutual understanding and saving time . . . I found the book fascinating'

B. Thompson-McCausland, Managing Director, National & Provincial

'A truly seminal work on the best decision support system there is: the human brain. A must for facing up to the human dimensions of Information Technology'

P. Laurence Traynor, Managing Director, Citation Consulting Ltd

'Colour-consciousness is now very much a part of my thinking, both within and outside my work . . . I feel as if I have been granted permission to be myself'

Jackie Kay, Senior Software Specialist, Prime Computer Inc

'Real education has never been merely cramming in knowledge. Especially today, children need to develop their thinking skills. This book gives me a practical conceptual base to build new learning projects. I found it challenging and exciting'

Alastair Sandiforth, Head of Sciences, Stanborough School, Welwyn Garden City

'Its language will become as much part of the vocabulary of management as concepts such as lateral thinking. If you're going to read only one book this month, let it be *The Colours of Your Mind*. Quite apart from what it may do for your future, it'll mean you won't be left out of the conversation at the next party you go to'

Prabhu Guptara, Management writer, lecturer and BBC broadcaster

'Having read your book, I am sure this approach could be very interesting to people in Therapy. Would it be possible for you to come and talk to us?'

June Langdon, Secretary, Society of Advanced Psychotherapy Practitioners

PRESIDENT   June 17th, 1988

Mr. J.D. Rhodes
Director Joint Development Resources
24 Cecil Park
<u>PINNER Middlesex HA5 5HH</u>
England.

Dear Mr. Rhodes,

"The Colours" has been on my table for quite a while and
if I have not answered you, it is because I had not read
it. In fact, this is still partly true. I am on my way,
though, and that means something. There is a daily
cavalcade of authors with brilliant new theories and we
approach them with rising suspicion.

However, someone challenging you to analyse your thinking
process, somehow catches the attention, if he reasons
leastways logically.

I find your book intriguing, the subject matter of prime
importance and the writing lively and amusing, forsooth,
not the least of virtues. I even have the stimulating
feeling that I am learning something.

Congratulations and kind regards,

                                    C.J. van der Klugt

Preface

In the course of writing this book we've often been pulled in different directions at the same time. Should we write a chapter better, or should we write a better chapter? – that is, write about some different aspect of the subject altogether. You ought to see the stuff we have scrapped! Have you ever seen a copy of G. K. Chesterton's delightful book, *The Coloured Lands*? The story goes that over the years his faithful secretary secretly rescued the jottings, sketches and manuscripts that Chesterton threw into the waste-paper bin. It was these throw-aways that enabled *The Coloured Lands* to be published after Chesterton's death, for he himself would not have thought such stuff worthwhile. We only hope that we have not thrown away all the good bits of this book!

One thing we are clear about: when you want to do something better, you start thinking. As we see it, thinking is purposeful. It has to do with **intention**. In a special way, therefore, it reflects motivation: whether you succeed or not may be a matter of luck, or availability of information, as well as of how capable you are, but anyone can try, even to write a book! We have set about it by signposting to ourselves the directions we have to take.

How far should we go to reach the highest possible quality? This is always a tough choice if you want standards of excellence and integrity. 'Nothing but the best is good enough' can sound wonderful, but can you deliver? The constant struggle to do better things better still is something we both feel deeply and hold very dear. Actually, it is a theme that's important in our book, because we try to give some practical ways in which people can improve their performance in all sorts of things.

But one constraint that might be quite real is how acceptable it will be to other people if you insist on going on and on towards 'excellence'. Maybe by making something too good you put it out of reach for many people. And this does not just mean a Hesketh motorcycle or a Rolls-Royce. As consultants we are always having to trade off quality against acceptability. There's nothing 'wrong' about that: it's just difficult. We have certainly felt the concern in writing this book not to blind people with science too much when the only way to get something absolutely right would be to risk that. So our approach has been to treat this tremendously complex subject of the mind as if we were learning to ski, on the nursery slopes. That meant taking things easily, trying the same things a number of different ways, lots of practice and some planned repeat runs. We hope that this will not make it all too unacceptable for the 'advanced skiers' who might read this, our first book on the subject.

The third part of our signpost was time. When it comes to making decisions, it seems to stand for all the other resources we had, including energy. So it is often the real arbiter between quality and acceptability. How long to spend, how often, at what intervals, by what date – the list goes on. One variation is 'How soon?' – which in Dutch is invariably expressed as 'How late?' In GKN managers used to be taught always to identify how late you could leave making a decision, and there's something in this. In Britain, we often prefer to delay making a big decision so that we won't make a wrong one, whereas the Americans will have made a decision and found it was wrong and corrected it and be onto the next project before we have got anything in place. So runs the mythology, anyway.

This 'How soon' question has actually faced us for years over the question when to publish our work. When could it ever be good enough to publish? Surely another year of experience and development, a few more hundred managers to test it out on and improve it . . . Then we remembered the famous saying of Alex Osborn, energetic promoter of the art of brainstorming, who wrote: 'Better an idea put to work than kept for ever on the polishing wheel.'

So that did it. We realize that when this book comes out we will wish we could instantly up-date it with all that we have discovered since sending it to the publisher. But it's like buying computers: you can always wait another year so as to get the most advanced technological miracles, but if you do, you never get any benefit at all. We're hoping people can't wait to read this book, either!

If so, it will be due in no small measure to our commissioning editor, Helen Fraser, who actually came to experience the ideas in a live session and has been more than positive in her support; and to our editor, Nadia Lawrence. Bob Garratt, too, we must thank for his encouragement and the critique he has given as someone who himself uses the Colours in his practice.

Our greatest tribute and warmest feelings must surely go to those fellow members of the project team in Philips, Eindhoven, who helped develop the core model of the Colours. It's impossible to convey the excitements and frustrations of our work as a team, the huge support we gave one another, the ways we 'ate our own bread', and the friendships that have endured over ten years now. First, Dr Hans Horeman and Dr Niek Wijngaards, who with Jerry Rhodes formed the original Three Musketeers, the core of the project. Later, Floris Timmer and Jan Ferdel Smit, who are doing more than anyone to achieve real results with the scientists and developers of R & D.

Our gratitude extends far beyond Philips, to all those clients who were willing to let us explore and develop and test the model on management programmes over several years. Chief among these have been Cliff Jacobsen, Reiner Olsson, Brian

McNicol and Alan Collinge, all at Shell International. And Ron Jackson, Ian Malcolm and John Cheese at National Westminster Bank. Among those who forced us to bring through some significant development in the Colours by asking us to do something fairly impossible, were Ben Thompson-McCausland of London Life, David Steel of Dunlop (now of Marconi), Jim Lynch of Barclays Bank, Graham Smith of the National Health Service, George Skomorowski of Kimberly-Clark and Jane Skinner of Aston University.

We have gained a lot from working in depth with our in-house coaches who pass on the mysteries of the Colours within their own organizations. Thanks are also due to the hundreds of Thinking Intention Profile participants who have given us permission to record their TIP questionnaire results on computer, for detailed analysis and research.

And now for friends, all the men and women and even children who have been willing guinea pigs in the name of all those who are not managers, just real people. Special friends too, like Ger and Dorothy Rietman in Holland, who have so often argued with us long into the night. And Rennie Fritchie who has been such a warm enthusiast for the Colours. Nearer home, there is Helen Levy who has done so much in improving the production of the book, in layout and illustrations, and especially her valuable critique of plain bewilderment or joyous wit. Finally, there's our close family who put up with our total hibernation over Christmas while we made the final revisions. We hope when they read the book they will understand why we told them our sacrifice was actually such fun.

Jerry Rhodes and Sue Thame
January 1987

CHAPTER ONE

Thinking

THE INVISIBLE

Isn't it amazing how often the most powerful and important things in life are invisible? Think of the invisible strength of love, courage, compassion. Insuperable odds are overcome by faith, hope and determination, like the US mission to put a man on the moon by 1970. Beliefs, like Liberty, Fraternity and Equality fuel revolutions that overturn society. Ideas, like Relativity, can open up a whole new universe. We see the *results* of invisible forces like these, but what *creates* them remains hidden in the mind. Being hidden in the mind, experienced but unseen, their power is somewhat feared, often avoided or denied and hardly comprehended. But things are changing in our times. The invisible forces of another revolution, information technology, are exposing our mental processes to an ever-increasing glare of investigation. This is prodding us all to become alert to learn about the mind-power that is so rapidly spreading over our planet. We invite you to become an explorer with us into the invisible world of the mind.

One major concern that has energized the research behind this book is the widespread opinion that thinking is abstract, having no real bearing on ordinary life, useful at school and for deskwork, paperwork, and little else. Any efforts you may have made to improve your thinking are probably associated with your childhood lessons, with college days, university, adult education, and most of all with exams. If so, it may not seem to have much to do with earning a living, or bringing up a family, or forming a successful relationship with a lover, a friend, a colleague.

The idea that thinking skills could help make a good marriage, a good job or a good social life or to achieve anything you want, might be seen as pretty doubtful. One of our aims is to dispel some of these educational hangovers which have caused the vast majority of people to pigeon-hole thinking into a category labelled 'Not For Me' or 'Cannot Do Much About'. We're going to look at the complete converse of that attitude, presenting the case that thinking is at the root of everything you do, even your relationships.

PERSONALITY MODELS

In recent years it has become fashionable to analyse one's personality through a variety of popular classifications. For example, many people can readily tell you whether they are an extrovert or an introvert. Almost everyone knows which astrological sign they were born under and what special character trait it reveals in them . . . Gemini is mercurial, Cancer is moody, Scorpio is passionate. Transactional Analysis has swept the world with Parent, Adult and Child type-casting. These popular short-hands on personality are common languages to convey to one another how we tick, very important in a fast-moving world where people change jobs and move around so rapidly. Indeed, such languages have been raised to professional status by people like Freud, with his concepts of ego, super-ego and id, and commercially translated into job selection and recruitment tests, like Jung's model of personality which has become the Myers Briggs Personality Inventory. Counselling programmes, like marriage guidance, clinical theology, co-counselling, have grown and developed since the 1950s, to help people increase their ability to recognize their behaviour patterns, to appreciate how they affect others, particularly those closest to them, so as to find ways to change the negative effects.

There are books galore showing you how to sell better, to manage better, to be a better leader, to be happier in your marriage and so on, based on personality and behaviour models of one kind or another. These models and the various jargons surrounding them provide special languages to describe the ways we behave with one another. Collectively, they have made a valuable contribution to the understanding of human interactions.

THINKING MODELS

In sharp contrast, when it comes to thinking there are very few such popular languages. De Bono's concept of lateral thinking has provided a useful way to talk about the creative part of mind. So also have Hudson's convergent and divergent problem-solving, and the left brain and right brain work of Ornstein. All these have opened up people's consciousness to their own thinking processes. Yet these three just about exhaust the list of well-known mind models, whereas an index of well-used personality models would stretch to several pages. There is a lot of room for developing the understanding of mind and thinking through models. This is what *The Colours of Your Mind* aims to do.

Now, there are some real barriers to getting people interested in all this mind stuff. Perhaps we should put it down to Descartes, who fostered the erroneous idea that Mind and Body are separate. This has led us to divide 'thinkers' from 'doers', rather to the detriment of each by the other. While 'thinkers' see themselves as superior contributors to society (usually with higher wages and better perks), 'doers' despise them as feeding off the wealth that they create at the 'coal-face' and on the shop-floor. In fact it is a little more complex than this.

Inspiration is seen to be on some sort of spiritual level. Thinking is on the level below and is usually taken to mean something like intellectual reasoning. Feelings and emotions are a bit carnal, and certainly to be subordinated to reason by any intelligent being. Doing is relegated to the Fourth Division!

Perhaps there is something realistic about this, for you could interpret Figure 1.1 as if it showed a sort of hierarchy, such as the class system in our society, levels of rank in the army,

1.1   Levels of mind – true or false?

INSPIRATION — god-like creatures who lead us

THINKING — academics and professionals

FEELING — women's work: 'emotional labour'

DOING — mindless labour

decision systems in the Civil Service, or the way a traditional manufacturing business organizes its people. You can trace hierarchies like this through the history of both Church and State and it goes back more than two thousand years, of course. In some countries, it seems to have widened the gulf between thinking and doing to such an extent that work of certain kinds cannot be contemplated by those who are too well educated. This happened in the golden century of Spain a few hundred years ago, when too many people went to universities and then considered themselves 'above it all'. It is repeated in Great Britain today, where 'the best people' don't even consider a career in industry, but go for the professions or aim to be the mandarins of the Civil Service. Commerce is considered acceptable if it is not too close to the market-place, and very close to the power of finance. And what of feelings, shifted onto the caring professions, staffed in the main by women, like nurses, social workers and nursery teachers?

The 'two cultures' notion seems to come in many forms, and is often perpetuated in the schools and universities, where of course most of the permanent inhabitants have never been lucky enough to work out in the world beyond. There, children and young people are driven to feel that exams and academic achievement are all that matter in education. What's worse, they are even forced to discriminate between arts and sciences, as if one were superior to the other. In Germany there is a more effective approach to promoting the integration of science and arts in schools, probably as a result of the attitudes of the culture where industrial managers are among the best educated in the land.

These ideas about the mind, that divide it up and box people into jobs which supposedly reflect the different parts, are patently too crude. Yet they have a grip on the popular imagination. It is quite wrong to see thinking as an activity pursued mainly by those who are clever or high up in the world. Thinking is required for the simplest of tasks if you want to do it well. Indeed it is quality of thought which separates the good labourer from the bad, the skilled craftsman from the indifferent, the effective manager from the ineffective. Everyone, especially in an advanced society, has to think and keep thinking better.

In our research we have followed a line of thought which enabled us to see thinking in a different light. We started by asking, how do you bring about the results you want to reach? Well, by your actions of course, what you *do*. Why do you do those actions unless you've reached the conclusion that it's the best way to get those results? It's a simple matter of cause and effect, isn't it? And those conclusions or thoughts are themselves brought about by thinking, the way you have used your mind to handle whatever information it could find.

Figure 1.2 is trying to show at least three things at once. Obviously, the strong cause-effect connection of thinking and doing. Secondly, that there is a real difference between thinking and thoughts. And finally, that by this definition thinking must embrace an awful lot more than the machinations of the intellect. This figure is claiming that everything you do or say is the result of thinking. What about feelings and emotions then? What about intuition? Where is the inspiration of the genius, and what about the sensitivity of the artist, poet, musician?

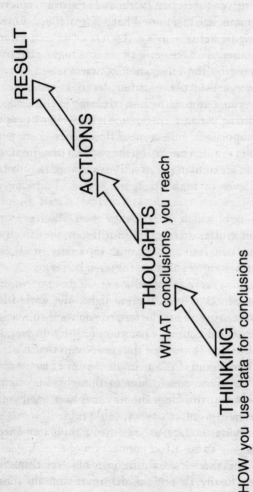

Figure 1 — Thinking Leads to Action

RESULT

ACTIONS

THOUGHTS
WHAT conclusions you reach

THINKING
HOW you use data for conclusions

Well, in Figure 1.2 all the attributes of mind are called 'thinking'. Instead of separating feelings, inspiration and intellectual thinking onto different levels, as in Figure 1.1, now they are all integrated into the same plane of 'thinking'. Once they are given an equal status, put on an equal footing as it were, you as a human being can make genuine choices between them instead of being tied down by some notion that they are automatically above or below one another. In other words, you can govern how you use your mind, making even-handed choices between using your emotions or your intellect or your senses or your imagination, and so on. Obviously this means 'thinking' takes on a much wider meaning than the narrow definition normally given to it.

THE LANGUAGE OF THE COLOURS

What we have tried to offer in our book is a different perspective on the mind, which comes from establishing a new language for dealing with thinking (in the widest sense). There are so many pressing reasons now why the majority of people should be able to understand how all day and every day they are using their minds to do things, and how by improving their thinking they can get things done better. A common framework, some new language, is needed through which everyone can convey how they are approaching a task. When you know what someone intends there is more chance of understanding what they say. You can help them make their contribution better, even if they are on the other side. What people do, their behaviour, can be better interpreted when you understand the thinking behind it.

Here in the Colours is a universal language which penetrates beneath behaviour to the thinking which drives us all. The Colours help you to read how someone's mind is really working – not least, your own! And the Colours' great advantage is that like all really useful tools for living they are easy to learn. They also cast an entirely new light on 'personality', and give a refreshing opportunity to go beyond and beneath the customary clichés used to interpret behaviour. This is because they create a different 'language' from that used by most 'psychological experts'. As the deep structure of behaviour is invisible it needs a language like the Colours, which is beyond overt behaviour, to interpret its meaning. Just as a scientist will turn to a different instrument or medium, ultra-violet or perhaps thermal photography, to penetrate what cannot be 'seen', so the Colours can reveal the significance of actions that cannot otherwise be observed.

With the Colours, thinking is made accessible to everyone. The Colours shine their light onto the invisible, revealing thinking processes in all their beauty and simple complexity. They make it possible to study thinking in its own right, not subsumed within the context of one or another specialist discipline to be absorbed only by some mysterious form of osmosis. In the Colours we can identify the thinking that is generic, common across disciplines and jobs, thus enabling transferable skills to be recognized in a much wider context. The time is ripe for thinking to be a subject in its own right! An ever-increasing proportion of people are now paid for their brain-power rather than their muscles, and companies compete to draw the best of the brainpower into their ranks. Good thinkers are in short supply and command premium salaries. They need to be developed in order for the demand to be met.

All the work on thinking which we have done over the past ten years has been helped enormously by the use of our special code of the Colours. The many men and women who have learnt about the Colours, and used them in their businesses, testify to the value of connecting thinking to effective action. Now it's time for more people to find this out for themselves.

How to Use this Book

Some people like books that allow them to have a solid read, even to study conceptual ideas without the interruption of too many examples and illustrations. Some read only on their journeys to and from work, so they want a book they can pick up and put down. Others like books that actively engage them, pencil in hand, in quizzes, questionnaires, puzzles, games, drawings and so on. Wit and humour are what attract other readers. Satisfying the requirements of all types in one book presents its difficulties, but we have tried.

1. Where to start

A fundamental tenet is that it is a practical necessity to know your own mind. So we strongly recommend that you find out your thinking style as soon as possible from Chapters Two and Three. It will give you a good operating base for exploring the rest of the book. One thing we must stress. Whatever thinking style you discover, it will only be a snapshot, taken in very unscientific circumstances. Don't allow yourself to become mesmerized by the picture that comes out. It is only an indicator, not an authority. Use it to give the Colours more personal meaning for you. As you make your way through the chapters, you will be able to bring the snapshot to life and breathe your own understanding into it.

2. Pick out the Colour code with coloured pens

The Colours of your thinking make your mind more visible to you. The Colours are a code or language invented to do the job that colour-coding does for a complex harness of electrical wiring, where it certainly matters which leads to connect with what. Colours make things easy to recognize. Right from the start, see if you can cast aside any natural reluctance to spoil the pristine pages of the book, and use coloured felt tips on it just as soon as you have discovered what the Colour Code is. *Not before*, for heaven's sake! Colour the figures and highlight the Colours in the text.

You should find that it's not only fun to do this, but a quick and practical way to get into the swing of it all. Colours can become tools of a special kind. They will give you a ready-made identification kit so that when you dip into your mental tool box you can pick out the appropriate tool quickly and accurately. You should find the Colours more than a simple shorthand: as you learn what they mean, you should get conceptual insights and understanding too. Try some felt pens!

3. Hold the conceptual thread

There is a solid and coherent argument through the book which, if treated at its conceptual level, allows you (if you have that turn of mind) to connect the underlying concepts here with your own ideas about what thinking is. However, you will find that the emphasis is not upon conceptual reasoning nor upon the fundamental research behind the Colours, but upon how to make use of it all.

If you are a travelling reader, there is enough segmentation in the book to allow for the breaks which will arise when your journey does not quite coincide with the length of the chapters. Do try to do each of the questionnaires in one bite without interruption, though. Otherwise you may spoil the value of the results.

4. Use the exercises for practice

There are plenty of exercises for those who like them. If this is not your cup of tea, you can skip them and still get to the meat of the book and make use of its ideas. But bear in mind that you will not improve your well-being by merely reading a book about fitness. You will certainly know more, but knowing does not of itself make you fitter. You've got to go and *do*. Since this book shows you how to improve the fitness of your thinking, the same applies. To develop your thinking you must take action. This involves reviewing your thinking habits, practising new ones and putting them to work in your life. So, to get you into the frame of mind for exercising, try this for starters.

Jot down a number of activities that you do at home and at work on some rough paper or in your diary. Sort them into four categories: I enjoy most . . . , I enjoy least . . . , I am best at . . . , I am worst at . . .

Try to be specific and aim to get five or six activities in each category. Be sure you have actually filled in the things you are best at. The exercise isn't asking, 'Are you the best among your colleagues at (giving presentations)?' No, it means of all your activities, which do you do best – and worst? You may find you don't necessarily like the activities you are best at or hate the ones you are worst at. Now put this exercise on ice until you can pick it up again in Chapter Five under 'Checking Your Own Thinking Style'. You will then be able to connect your likes and dislikes, your bests and worsts, to the Colours and to your own thinking style.

5. Try out the models and maps

The first few chapters describe a model of thinking and a variety of associated concepts, enabling you to label a range of mental activities in a language that will be totally new to you. Get the hang of it by using it, at first on your own.

In the middle of the book you can find out how to make use of what you are learning, especially with other people. See how the models and the language of Colours actually work.

When you come to the final chapters you will be ready to explore how the Colours could make for more effectiveness in managing your work. Difficult tasks can be 'mapped', in Colours, so that it is more obvious how you should tackle them. Since 'Maps' contain many levels of complexity, they cannot be fully treated here, but you should get the broad idea how to make use of them. Start at a very simple level, not expecting too much from a 'rule of fist' approach. Chapter Nine shows you how.

6. Application

Those who are alert and eager to learn should get the kind of insights into their thinking skills that will enable them to modify some of their ways of handling common work activities. You can compare what you read with your own experience and raise the standards you set for your own performance. You can do some simple tests of your understanding with the people you deal with and notice how this grows or deepens as time goes on. We hope that when you've finished the book you will want to read it again, to encourage colleagues and friends to read it, and to explore further the methodology that underlies the Colours.

7. Research background

We have written the book as much as possible in plain English, giving plenty of examples to illustrate our meaning. The work is grounded in robust research with the pragmatic aim of helping people think better in their jobs and relationships. But do not let the simplicity fool you into thinking either that this book is simplistic or that the work presented here is of the genre of a quick fix to transform your thinking. The Colours represent a massive and useful simplification of work done over many years on many levels of complexity. In this book, you will find only the first and second levels of the model of thinking. A brief account of the research background and the other levels can be found in Chapter Ten.

8. The basic theme of the book runs like this:
   a) Skilful thinking is invisible, unrecognized but absolutely central to all other skills.
   b) Awareness of the natural resources of mind is essential for increasing effectiveness in action.
   c) A model like the Colours, showing the anatomy of mind, makes its various functions understandable. Although it is a metaphorical model, it serves the essential purpose of making tangible a whole field of activity that is generally seen as unnecessarily vague and abstract. It raises awareness.
   d) This awareness is the first stride towards conscious control, direction, steering and improvement of thinking.

e) By distinguishing *how* thinking is done from *what* thoughts people have, everyone can use the same model for thinking processes, the same language or code to illuminate, explain and understand one another's thoughts. This book would not presume to suggest what you should think, simply how. Awareness of the range of Colours open to you will enhance the quality of the freedom you enjoy in choosing what to do.

f) People tend to see tasks according to their own thinking style. Only if they are aware of the influence of this style on their perceptions can they adjust the way they naturally value things like time, information, ideas and values, so as to match what the task actually requires of them.

g) There is no ideal thinking style. People with different thinking styles, knowing how they differ, will bring themselves to bear more effectively on a complex situation than people with notionally 'ideal' styles.

CHAPTER TWO

Unveiling the Colours of Your Mind

In Chapter One you will have picked up the gist of our approach to thinking. In essence, the Colours give you access to the inner workings of your mind, and even into the minds of other people. Like musical or mathematical notation, which is international, the symbolic Colour-code of Mind replaces words because it can transcend the barriers of language and specialisms. We want to give you access to this code so that you can absorb it and turn it to good use for yourself. So we are immediately throwing you in at the deep end, and without any further explanations or apologies we want you to find out the Colours of your mind: your thinking style. We hope you haven't browsed through too much of the book yet, since this might disturb the innocence of your approach to the questionnaires that follow. If you have, just try to be as honest as you can in your replies.

The quickest way for you to get hold of the Colour-code is to make use of the questionnaires we have designed in this chapter and the next. Normally, when working 'live', we administer a carefully researched inventory, so as to arrive at a detailed profile that characterizes each person individually. As we obviously cannot give you our normal feedback on the results, we have worked out a simpler method just for this book. It will be enough to give you the essential grasp you need to start with. Then, as you go through the other chapters and as your understanding develops, you will have lots of chances to check out your thinking style. Have a go at the questionnaire that follows.

Charting the Colours of Your Thinking

So that you clearly understand how to do this, read through this briefing before answering any of the questions that follow.

It is important that you respond with what you like and enjoy in an order of preference, not what you think *ought* to be. This will reflect your natural preferences, not what you may be forced into by your education or your job.

However the questions may be phrased, be aware not to respond with what you actually do, nor how you think others see you. Those scores might be very different, so don't muddle them up. Later, you may want to repeat this Charting exercise three or four times from different perspectives – such as, how your partner sees you – and compare the results.

A FEW WORDS OF ADVICE

* It is better to do the Charting first, before you read about how to interpret the Colour-code. If you jump the gun and read up on the Colour-code first, it could affect your perceptions of yourself thus prejudicing the way you go about completing the Chart. If so, your answers could be less authentic.

* Allow yourself 10 to 15 minutes to answer all the questions at one sitting.

* Don't spend ages over it. Be spontaneous. The first response that comes into your head may well be the most authentic. But as each of the three options in each block is subtly different from the next, don't be too glib either. Just make sure you are not responding to some 'professional' persona in yourself which dictates 'oughts'. This Chart is for what you *like* to do.

* There are no wrong answers. All answers are right if they are true to yourself.

* A few people may feel uncomfortable at the thought of being pigeon-holed by the Chart and reluctant to complete it.

Don't cut yourself off from the option: you will need to refer to this Chart as you go through the book. First impressions can only happen once.

* Do write in this book. Your markings will make it much more personal and useful, turning it into your own work book. Later on, we will even encourage you to use coloured pens. Although our education actually forbade us to violate such a holy thing as the printed page, we find that to do so is really an enhancement. Like tools, books are to be used rather than kept clean under a cover. If you find this advice hard to act on, your Colour Chart may later give some hints as to why this is so.

Now, have a go.

The Colour Chart

There are 48 statements below, in 16 blocks of three. Each block of three statements should be treated as one unit to be answered together.

In each block of three, score the statements according to your preference by distributing 10 points between them. Always deal in whole numbers. Here are some examples of possible ways to score your distribution. They are not exhaustive, just samples.

At one extreme, if you preferred one statement to the complete exclusion of the other two, you would score:	10 0 0
If you liked them all about equally, you would score:	3 4 3
If you liked one a lot and didn't feel strongly about the other two, you would score:	6 2 2

At another extreme, if you hated one and   0
liked two a lot you would score: 5
   5

*You must score all three in each block, making sure to distribute
all 10 points between them.*

START HERE

Score

BLOCK ONE
 	
If I could choose the problems I had to tackle, my preference would be to:
  1. Investigate something that has gone wrong.
  2. Think up all sorts of possible ways to achieve an outcome.
  3. Evaluate the best way forward from a number of possibilities.
	
	. . .
	
	. . .
	
	. . .

BLOCK TWO
 	
In meetings I am happiest when:
  4. Persuading someone to change their view and agree with my opinions.
  5. Working out just how to put something across and getting the chance to communicate it really well.
  6. Coming up with a touch of inspiration that gives my approach a kind of uniqueness or competitive edge.
	
	. . .
	
	. . .
	
	. . .

BLOCK THREE

If I were candid about the kind of influence I like to exert, it is really to do with:

7. Getting people to follow me in what I see as best. . . .
8. Casting around and coming up with new ideas or new angles which lead by their originality. . . .
9. Making sure that people get to the genuine unvarnished truth of the matter, with as little bias or prejudice as possible. . . .

BLOCK FOUR

For me, much the most important way to handle an issue is to:

10. Have a clear statement of all the facts and figures needed to deal with it accurately. . . .
11. Ensure that the argument is coherently and soundly put together so that the logic is foolproof. . . .
12. Get away from the assumptions and constraints of the past so as to open up people's minds to ringing the changes. . . .

BLOCK FIVE

If I am going to buy something:

13. I keep my mind open for opportunities and delightful surprises. . . .
14. It's better for me if I systematically find out what products are available before firming up what I want. . . .
15. I won't even start until I have sorted out what I really want from it. . . .

BLOCK SIX

When we are planning an event, the bit I like best is:

16. Making all those difficult choices about what we should and should not do.   . . .

17. Dreaming up all the things that could go wrong and what to do instead.   . . .

18. Making the lists and detailed arrangements for the preparations.   . . .

BLOCK SEVEN

The best way for me to deal with an argument or some other conflict is to:

19. Seek a way out that is so ingenious it takes the others by surprise and reveals an entirely new dimension.   . . .

20. Try to prove a water-tight rationale, and show how well my case makes sense.   . . .

21. Find out what information we have in common and what is different between us, perhaps looking for a more suitable form of expression.   . . .

BLOCK EIGHT

In times of pressure or crisis, I am in my element when:

22. Coming down to things that matter.   . . .

23. Getting at what needs to be known and putting that across.   . . .

24. Coming up with an unusual angle on the subject.   . . .

BLOCK NINE

The kind of question I most like to raise:

25. Challenges the established wisdom of what most people normally think.   . . .
26. Ensures that a line of argument is logically watertight.   . . .
27. Switches perspectives from looking inside the issue to its background context.   . . .

BLOCK TEN

When I need to plan, I like to start with:

28. Taking stock and looking at all the data I can easily lay my hands on.   . . .
29. Feeling my way into the scene, listening to any hunches and intuitions.   . . .
30. Coming out with my view of what is sure to happen on the way through the plan.   . . .

BLOCK ELEVEN

When something goes seriously wrong and we need to know why, what I take most care about is:

31. Ensuring that we compare things properly, like with like.   . . .
32. Assembling all the complete data, without fear or favour.   . . .
33. Coming up with all the possibilities, not just the most obvious.   . . .

BLOCK TWELVE

For me, the hallmark of a good written proposal is:

34. The unexpected and even brilliant connections that are made for the first time.   . . .
35. In the long and the short of it, how well it interprets the situation.   . . .
36. Whether the style and format is designed to make the message clear to the people it is aimed at.   . . .

BLOCK THIRTEEN

When anyone asks me to do something for them, I like it best when:

37. They tell me the scale of it – roughly right but fast, or in detailed perfection.   . . .
38. I have to find my own ways around awkward aspects of the task.   . . .
39. They tell me what matters to them, and ensure I can work with the same kind of aims.   . . .

BLOCK FOURTEEN

Whenever I have to gather information on some subject or other, the one thing I make sure of is:

40. Identifying and naming the main headings.   . . .
41. Putting it together in a variety of ways in the hope of new angles emerging.   . . .
42. Comprehensive research through detailed, tight questioning.   . . .

BLOCK FIFTEEN

If I have to persuade someone, the part that most appeals to me is:

43. Keeping an open mind so as to pursue all the possible alternatives for reaching agreement. . . .
44. Gathering in, marshalling and laying out the information much more effectively. . . .
45. Timing when to cut the cackle and go firm on something, big or small. . . .

BLOCK SIXTEEN

When I'm really operating on top form:

46. My mastery of the subject matter is so specific and complete that the conclusions follow naturally. . . .
47. I am so confident of my judgement there's little need for better information or ideas. . . .
48. My genius shows in plenty of brilliant ideas and I'm willing to let others work out the details and draw the obvious conclusions for action. . . .

Transfer your scores into the columns of the Score Chart below, putting the scores next to the appropriate numbers. When you have entered them all, add up the three individual columns and put the totals below. Every number should have a score, even if it is 0.

SCORE CHART

3 . . .	1 . . .	2 . . .
4 . . .	5 . . .	6 . . .
7 . . .	9 . . .	8 . . .
11 . . .	10 . . .	12 . . .
15 . . .	14 . . .	13 . . .
16 . . .	18 . . .	17 . . .
20 . . .	21 . . .	19 . . .
22 . . .	23 . . .	24 . . .
26 . . .	27 . . .	25 . . .
30 . . .	28 . . .	29 . . .
31 . . .	32 . . .	33 . . .
35 . . .	36 . . .	34 . . .
39 . . .	37 . . .	38 . . .
40 . . .	42 . . .	41 . . .
45 . . .	44 . . .	43 . . .
47 . . .	46 . . .	48 . . .
TOTALS		
BLUE	RED	GREEN

THE THREE COLOUR CHART

Put your totals from your score chart into these boxes:

Totals

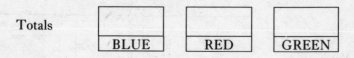

| BLUE | RED | GREEN |

Using colour pencils or felt pens, Blue, Red and Green, make your own Colour Chart with your scores (Figure 2.2).

Be sure you get the Colours in the right places. (See the three examples in Figure 2.1 where we have used shading to simulate the three Colours.)

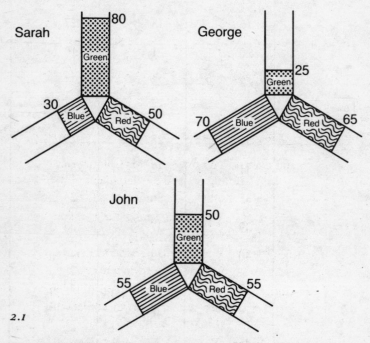

2.1

First, a quick guide to interpreting your Chart.

The Chart shows you a snapshot picture which gives clues about the ways in which you habitually tend to think, because it reflects which Colours you most like to use, and which least.

2.2

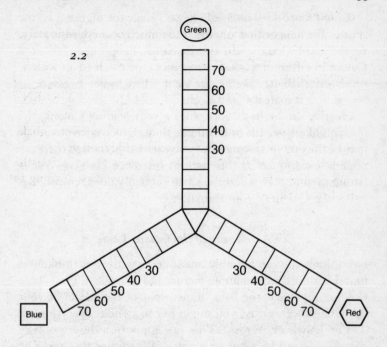

70 and over	You over-use this Colour, relying on it to the detriment of the other Colours.
61–69	You often lead your thinking with this Colour.
50–60	You should be able to use this Colour as and when needed.
41–49	This Colour will tend to be an also-ran in your vocabulary of thinking skills.
40 and under	You probably avoid this Colour, maybe to the point of neglect.

A high score does not mean 'good', since the higher it is, the greater the danger that you use it too much or inappropriately, regardless of what the situation demands. People use a favoured Colour in different ways. For instance, you can lead off with it, finish off with it, take refuge in it when under pressure or attack, flog it to death, and so on.

Clearly, the highest score will be your leading Colour, the one you like best, the one you like to use given a free hand. It may be the one you are most effective with too, though there are notable exceptions to this natural inference. It gives you a strong card to play when the situation really does require that particular Colour of your thinking.

The Meaning of the Colour Code

Everything you can possibly intend to do with your thinking is found within the one simple picture in Figure 2.3. The Three Colours represent the basic dimensions of the whole of your thinking processes. As you might say to a child, everything is 'Up or Down or Across'. This can apply to a description of simple objects like a box or a piece of furniture that must be carried up some narrow stairs, but also to advanced mathematical concepts like topology or the construction of maps, models or holographs. The analogy of dimension may be particularly apt, as you will see that the Colour you adopt at any one moment represents the direction you intend to drive towards with your thinking.

This simplicity contains deeper levels of complexity which will gradually be explained, but to begin the exploration of your mind you need only remember these Three Colours. It will help the visual recall of all the diagrams if you colour them yourself with pencils or felt pens.

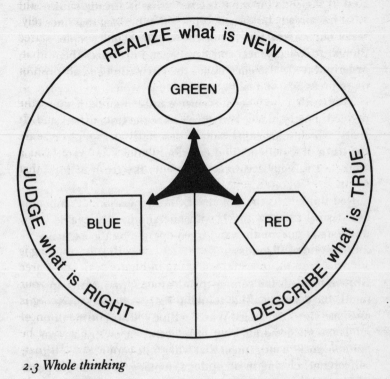

2.3 Whole thinking

THE DISTINCTIVE QUALITIES OF THE THREE COLOURS

Green is the code for the unknown, the as-yet-unrealized future, the possibilities that may or may not materialize. When you are Green you are uncommitted to action, just using your mind to throw ideas around which you may or may not pick up and use. All new ideas spring from Green thinking. It is divergent, lateral, imaginative, intuitive, unformed, crazy, odd, out-of-the-ordinary; upsetting convention, disturbing habits, playing with possibilities. Green thinking does not fit what is already established, because it is seeking to create what doesn't yet exist. Green thinking disturbs the status quo, and so unfortunately can go off at half-cock and be misunderstood and suppressed. But Green is also fun and the fountain of creativity.

Red is the code for 'what is true', what is already known and what has already happened. This is the thinking that finds out, seeks out information about the world, about people, about things. It collects facts and figures, and organizes them in an orderly way. It also encourages the circulation and absorption of impressions of reality, impressions which are needed to convey truth, even when it is elusive and cannot be measured or defined. Poetry, dance and novels have the Colour Red at their roots, which finds expression in descriptive images to convey the truth of experience and emotion. Quite a different face of truth lies in your accounts statement: the truth of measurement.

Red thinking is the Colour of communication. It embodies our desires to be in touch with one another, to enable us to understand one another and to co-operate by the exchange of information of all kinds.

Blue is the code for 'coming to judgement', for making up your mind, for deciding. Blue thinking makes choices, gives opinions, has views on things. When in Blue you are cutting through information, deciding what is relevant, in order to form an opinion, make a judgement that will guide your actions. Blue is convergent, closing in on options, moving to the single point where a decision can be made. It requires personal values and beliefs to be brought to bear in choices, yet uses a framework of logic and straightforward reasoning to do so.

We get things done through Blue thinking. It draws Red and Green together, commanding them to its purpose, determining what kinds of idea and information will be relevant. Then Blue must weigh it all up and precipitate action.

INTENTION

Each Colour covers a different aspect of your deep thinking intentions. They are like objectives. You choose which Colour to use according to what you want to achieve from your thinking. When you choose one you turn your back on the other two, because you are seeking something neither of them can give you. When you look at Figure 2.3, imagine you keep starting from the neutral position in the middle, then going outwards along one of the three arrows of force. This is always happening, but people aren't usually conscious that they are using their minds in this way.

Here are some quick questions to establish what you are really driving at in your thinking:

Am I aiming   to get a new approach?
               to discover a new possibility?
               to find a new idea?
               to break out of old habits?

If so, your thinking is being driven by Green intentions, represented by the ellipse.

Am I trying   to find out what is going on?
               to tell what information is available?
               to elicit what people know?
               to get down facts and figures?

Then you are being driven by Red intentions, represented by the hexagon.

Am I seeking   to form an opinion on things?
               to persuade myself or someone else about what is sound?
               to interpret other views and opinions?
               to evaluate effectiveness or quality?

Then you are being driven by your Blue intentions, symbolized by the square.

Of course you can ask similar questions of other people too, in order to clarify their real intentions.

When you are thinking, you always operate from one of the Three Colours. Whatever thoughts you have will spring from a deep intention either to **Realize** some new idea, or to **Describe** information that is true, or to **Judge** someone or something. Having worked with hundreds of managers as they were introduced to the Three Colours, we know what first reactions to expect to this bald statement. There are always some who feel at first that it cannot be valid. Others, that it is too obvious for words. So there must be something right about it! But they quickly resolve their diverse objections when they begin to put the Colours into practice. The three words in bold type do have a wealth of meaning, of course. Please see them as a special jargon, a shorthand technical description for our purposes.

> 'It means whatever I say it means'
> – Lewis Carroll

The point will become clearer when we tell you that each Colour includes both an active and a passive approach. For instance, when in Red the objective is Truth. Whether you are aiming to tell the truth or to ask for it you are using the Red part of your mind. Whether you are doing the talking or the listening, the giving or the receiving, the knowing or the finding out. All of this is called Describe in our shorthand, and to call it Red makes it a more obviously coded use of language.

In the same way, when the objective is wisdom or rightness as distinct from truth, you may want either to judge something or to persuade, that is, to cause someone else to receive your judgement and change their own. No one can allow persuasion even to begin until they are willing to aim for what is right. So it is equally apt that both kinds of judging are seen as Blue. The implications of this for satisfactory argument and discussion begin to appear at once of course.

In similar vein, when trying to Realize new ideas, which we call a Green intention, there are again two aspects: the active search for ideas, and the apparently more passive state of mind reflecting a willingness to receive and welcome insights from wherever.

	SENDING OUT	RECEIVING IN
Red	tell	ask/listen
	show	see/feel
Blue	persuade	evaluate
Green	seek/search	welcome insight

People commonly confuse the ideas of Right and True. They muddle these rather in the same way that they are apt to muddle opinions with statements, what they can only judge with what they actually know, interpretations with observations, and so on. At first it may not be clear that what is new is the natural enemy of what is already known as 'true', and even more in conflict with the established concepts on which judgement is naturally based.

Because of the peculiar nature of Green thinking, the active and passive take a different but comparable form. When you Realize, in our terms, you could either actively be trying to reach a realization, or receiving a realization (as when an idea comes to you). In the latter case, it is not just a matter of 'hearing' something from the heavens, but actively 'listening'. So you see that words like active and passive do not perfectly describe these two-directional approaches. Moreover, Green has no natural component for dealing with people, as is the case with Red and Blue. The nature of ideas and having them has this ineffable quality which seems to rise above people and can give problems, as we will see.

The Colours are your fundamental intentions, the basic drives of your thinking, which operate sometimes consciously but more often below your consciousness, affecting the direction your mind will take. These Three Colours cover, at a deep level, all your thinking impulses. From these Three Colours spring all your thoughts. That last sentence may sound a bit bombastic or pretentious, as if we were claiming that when in Green you were bound to get an inspiration, when in Red you could guarantee to actually speak or discover the truth, when in Blue you were always right. Not so. The Colours, and the whole model of thinking operations that emerged from our research, are about what you are aiming for, not whether you hit it; that is, they show your inner intentions, not necessarily the results that show in the world outside. Of course there is a connection, or else there would be little point in exploring the invisible level below what can be observed. The connection is of fundamental cause and effect.

*

Just think what happens when as a customer you ask the shop assistant about the performance of some equipment you are about to buy, a stereo system perhaps. Naturally you are asking for Red information. The assistant may tell you about it, in Red, with no intention to deceive, and yet the information could easily be incomplete, inaccurate and if not specifically untrue, at least misleading. You then fail to buy it, and perhaps go elsewhere and buy something else, to discover the mistake only later.

The assistant may well have been in her best Red, but she was new and inexperienced and so did not actually possess the truth required to deliver the result she was honestly aiming at. We say 'honestly' because it is impossible to be dishonest in Red . . . because the Colours are about **intentions**. In seeking information about the stereo, can you imagine ever actually wanting to be told what is untrue? How about having a telephone directory full of wrong numbers? It would be absurd.

Who knows most about that stereo system's performance? The salesman from the manufacturers of course. As a specialist from, let's say a mythical company called Audiotronics Ltd, he can make the thing sit up and beg, can tune it to the acoustics from the furnishings of your drawing room, knows every detail of its comparison with other manufacturers' equipment, and also each one of its shortcomings with infinite pain! Had he been in the shop that day, you could have had the gen from the horse's mouth. And yet, and yet. . . .

What may be in your mind is that sometimes people actually do wish to mislead, and even to be misled. To take the latter first, it is indeed possible to prefer not to know. Perhaps the doctor has to recognize this with certain patients, the expert with certain managers, the lawyer or accountant at certain moments. There are more people in the world who would prefer a portrait showing them in their best light than did Oliver Cromwell, who demanded to be painted 'warts and all'. But when you don't want the truth, you are not in Red, you are in Blue. You are being influenced by your values, allowing your judgement to come into it. Sometimes scientists do not like the results of their experiments because they fail to bear out the conclusion they had hoped for. If you are on a quest for reality but try to influence outcomes, you are lost.

Take the example of the salesman from Audiotronics Ltd. He has a vested interest in your buying his brand of stereo equipment. When he gives you information, might he not want to tell you a lie, or massage the truth, or at least leave something out that he knows would be damaging? Well, this can be a dilemma. But as soon as bias, prejudice, vested interest, values and personal subjective perceptions can be recognized as being in operation, Red truth is in danger. A good salesman knows this and resolves it, both for himself and for his customer. It may be more of a problem for his customer than for him. The customer may be so obsessed with his assumption that he will be given a biased story by a salesman that he could over-compensate, mistrust facts and figures that are accurate and genuine, even understated. He is then in Blue while his salesman is in Red. Result: disaster!

The difference between intention and result is nowhere more obvious than when you are using your Green mind, reaching out for a solution to your problem. Here it is clear that your intention to search for an idea may not be rewarded by the flash of recognition you hope for. How can anyone be sure of inspiration? Less obviously, the product of any Green thinking may not actually be new, in the sense that no one else has ever thought of it before. It may not be a good idea, either. And indeed hours of wrestling with a problem in your mind may not actually result in a useful end-product. Yet you have been in Green, because your intention was to seek the unusual, a new angle on things, a way out or a competitive edge.

Look back at Figure 1.2 in Chapter One. Now that you know about your own Chart, you can see the importance of the deepest level, which can be seen as driving the whole chain: the Colours of your Mind are at the root of the process which leads to action and results.

Everyone has a different mixture of the Three Colours,

causing them to think in different ways from one another. Someone who has a preference for Red with little Blue and even less Green will use their mind in very different ways from someone who is high on Green, with little Red, and less Blue. This can be advantageous and it can be disastrous: it depends how well they handle their Colours in different situations. Much more of this later, but first you will need a little more detail on what the Colours mean, and how to read your scores.

CONFLICT OF DIRECTION

People's intentions fundamentally affect how they set about doing things and how they respond to other people. If they have a bias to one Colour they will usually lead with it, regardless of the situation they are in. It will be the first way they react. They will use that Colour when things really matter. Or it will be their habitual mental stance, much as people adopt habitual postures . . . so you can always recognize someone you know well just from the way they walk, stand or sit, without seeing the detail of their whole body.

Figure 2.3 shows how the three energies for achieving originality, truth and rightness are naturally driving out in opposed directions. We have to measure truth by what is already known, what we can see and feel and measure. It appears in the form of evidence, that which can literally be verified. (*Veritas* is Latin for truth.) It needs to be in some recognizable form, so that we can name it, catalogue it, put it in some pigeon-hole of our memory. All this makes Red at odds with both Blue and Green, but in different ways.

Green energy looks for things that are new and original. For Green it is a plus point that nothing is known. If it were already well known and commonly observed, as is the way with Red, it wouldn't be new, would it? Indeed, Green often sets about getting new ideas simply by taking what already is and then violating it, changing one or more of its existing parameters. You want a new kind of watch? All right, why not hang it upside down? Bound to be useful for someone: an acrobat perhaps, or how about a hospital nurse? (Incidentally, it might be interesting to pursue the reason why more people do not wear a watch like that. It's highly convenient in some ways, and possibly a nice line in jewellery!)

Blue energy favours the closing mind. Blue knows what it likes and uses this confidence in judgement to override all else when the chips are down. Blue dictates to Red which kinds of information matter, and is apt to ignore data that do not fit this prescription. 'I see what I want to see, I reject what I don't believe. The figures must be wrong if they don't conform to my formula. If there isn't time to get the full information, I will make up my mind anyway. Don't confuse me with more facts: I have already made up my mind.' Imagine what this patrician and imperious attitude does to the pride of Red. Red energy is devoted to seeking and providing the best possible information, the more the merrier. Red is willing to serve the imperious demands of Blue, but like any good servant is miffed when there is no time to enjoy the dinner it has so carefully prepared.

Green energy has already been shown as living on the violation of Red facts. From Green's point of view at least, this is done with good humour, in the cause of reaching for a new version of reality. One meaning of the word Realize is to reach a new reality, one that is beyond what is already visible. Such an attitude can be anathema to Blue. Blue has its value-system, and is subject also to the rule of law in the form of logic and reason. Blue can approve only of things that conform to such absolute canons of 'rightness'. This upstart young fellow called Green is not to be tolerated but rather brought to heel firmly. 'There is nothing good about your new idea because it challenges what we have always believed.' What infuriates Blue is that the Green approach is uncommitted, for when you start having a new idea, you cannot be restricted by the need for it to be a *good* one or the idea will be still-born, or die in the throat. So Green operates at first with a delightful freedom from either truth (Red) or rightness (Blue). This can be offensive enough to a Red, but it is downright immoral to a Blue. From the other side, Green can often feel impatient with the insistence on realism and accuracy that comes from Red, and thoroughly oppressed by the rejection of any innovation by Blue.

From all this, it might look as if the Colours can never co-operate, because each has a fundamental drive away from the others. Were it not for the magic of human sociability we would all be shooting off in different directions except when by chance we landed on the same Colour at the same time. Unfortunately, we *are* often in different Colours from one another. Then no one seems to be able to communicate with anyone else, and meetings get nowhere. But human capacity for synergy of difference can bring about collaboration between the Colours, producing harmony and a whole that is greater than the sum of the parts. The most dynamic and fruitful marriages and business partnerships can be based on this principle – as long as each person recognizes and understands that the mind of the other operates fundamentally differently.

This difference between all the Colours means you can operate with tremendous flexibility if you are able to value each approach for its particular contribution. Once you know that your mind works in these different ways you can tune yourself more finely to its moods, its wanderings, its machinations, its confusions, so that you control it or let it go free, to match the situation that confronts you.

DRIVING FORCES

Generally speaking, most people have a dominant or a driving Colour (the top score of your Chart). If so, you can think of the others as either the supporting back-up or the trailing or neglected Colour (your lowest score). (See Figure 2.4.)

The implications of these different patterns in different people are legion. Later on, we will discuss in more depth the effects of the driving Colours on your relationships with people, and in your work. Actually, all the Colours operate to a greater or lesser extent all the time. You seldom have a purely Green intention, without Blue or Red playing into it. It is useful to look at the Colours as separate entities, but remember that they

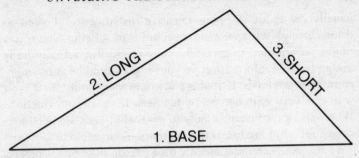

2.4 Driving forces triangle

always exist together, both in our minds and the tasks we address. None of the Colours is ever completely missing. There is always a kaleidoscope effect, as one shades finely into another, or as one level of Colour overlays or is woven into another.

It is significant on a practical level to recognize which is the base or driving Colour, and in what order the other two are driven. Be aware too of the triangle of forces. Blue driving Red driving Green is different from Blue driving Green driving Red. Often your mind seems to change its triangle of forces spontaneously, but you can take control and decide. It is also essential to recognize how someone else is operating his triangle.

For example, if you are predominantly Green and your boss walks in saying, 'Got any ideas on what we can do about shipping those sensitive instruments?' you will probably respond without difficulty, because your mind naturally likes playing with ideas. And as long as your boss is not expecting only good ideas – that is, only ideas that will work – then your mind can play around, throwing up all sorts of crazy notions, confident that if you think up enough of them, one will lead to something useful. A boss who values you for your Green will make effective use of your natural talent.

But what if the situation requires another Colour? If you are sufficiently aware, you will respond appropriately. But if the Colour required is a low scorer for you, you may duck the issue. This time, the boss walks in saying, 'Tell me, what do we usually do about shipping sensitive instruments? I need to think through what we should do in future.' Being Green you might be tempted to give him your ideas. But actually he is asking for Red information, so your ideas would be annoyingly counter-productive. If Red is a low scorer on your Chart, you won't be very switched on by his need for plain information. When anyone constantly fails to give what another person is asking for, they are brewing a contentious situation.

In the same circumstances, a Blue person might have picked up only the second part of the boss's question, because for Blue what *should be* overwhelms what *is* the way we normally ship them. So he may come up with a rationale showing why the current way is no good, or begin blaming particular aspects of the shipping procedures, or even plumping for a better procedure which he likes, without checking all the facts. The boss has in fact given two messages, a Red one followed by a Blue, because he plans to get facts before making any judgements. But Blue people tend to jump to Blue conclusions too quickly.

Knowing your Driving Force Triangle (or someone else's) helps. People usually develop real skills with the favoured Colours because they are exercising those particular mental muscles more than the others. This reinforces their preference and causes them to rely even more on their driving Colours, so that the range of their Process capability tends to become contained. This means that whatever situation they meet they always tackle it from the same pattern of Process, or grouping of thinking intention Colours. If your small son gets only one tool for Christmas, a hammer, he might treat everything he sees as a nail!

We have already seen that someone who is Green will tend to approach all situations with a drive to make new connections. They will say things like 'We could add this to . . .', 'This is like . . .', 'I can see a possibility of . . .', 'There's a link here with . . .', 'Do we really have to stick to these constraints?', 'I'll bet we can find a way out of this', 'Suppose we took another angle altogether . . .', 'How else could we do it?'

At a subtle level we see that the power of the Driving Force colours the way the other Colours are used. In the case of this Green person for example, the power of the Green will colour the way in which they use their Blue and Red. Even when they are seeking to reach the truth (in Red) the quality of their Green exploratory mind will be present and insert itself into the Red activity. Their Green underpins their Red – and may overbear it. For example, they might say, 'They are building a new supermarket in the middle of our suburban village,' (Red); and then go on to liken the project with the M25 motorway round London (Green), 'It'll be just the same sort of thing, attracting traffic from all over the place that never travelled that way before. Solid traffic jams and the ruination of life for miles.'

By giving the analogy they immediately underpin their Red statement with a Green connection, whereas someone whose driving force is Red may simply make the statement and add more facts, such as how big the supermarket will be and when it is due to be finished, without making such an unusual connection. (It must be unusual, because in neither case did all those clever planners make it!)

In both cases, for the Red and the Green person, their Driving Intention is to be Red, to tell the truth, but the Green person adds the quality of his Greenness to the Red statement. So you will find that Green people use a lot of analogies or illustrations to put their points across whereas Red people will stay closer to the immediate reality of what they wish to convey. Of course, we all know that this is the very stuff of personality. The intermixing of habits of mind (Process) with the experience (Data) of an individual's life, forms the unique colour of a personality.

PROCESS V. DATA

In this book we may sometimes use the words Data and Process in a way that is not familiar to everyone reading it. Briefly, Data will be used to cover ideas, information and values that can be treated as 'thoughts', whereas Process will be used to mean the way data is handled. Data means *what* you know, Process means *how* you get it and deal with it. To stretch for analogy from language itself, Data is more like nouns, subjects, and objects, Process more like verbs. It is then easier to see Data as including both the raw materials and the products of the thinking-factory of your mind, whereas Process represents whatever goes on in that thinking-factory to collect the raw materials and convert them into finished products. It is the Process that 'adds the value'. And the directions and routes and procedures of your mental factory are driven by your intentions, which colour everything you approach (Figure 2.5).

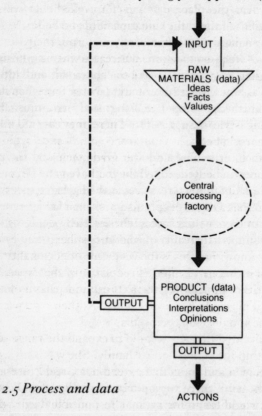

2.5 Process and data

Many people become aware as they grow older that their range of ability is becoming limited and they take quite deliberate steps to extend themselves. Some take a new job which makes new demands on their thinking. These new demands are not just new Data (selling washing machines instead of televisions). They are really shifting the thinking Process demands of their jobs: for example, from selling to marketing, production to personnel, audit to consultancy, though they may stay with the same company. Of course, the Data will change too, but this will be determined by the Process. The Driving Force of any job can be identified through Colour Analysis. People looking for work will find this opens out new areas of their thinking capacities and helps them select something suitably different.

Another aspect of career change is noticeable when someone reaches a ceiling on the way up his or her chosen ladder. Since more senior jobs often require Colour driving forces quite different from what was appropriate at the more junior levels, a person's thinking style may not fit. There may be all the difference in the world between a junior accountant and a senior manager in finance, or between a lower grade technical and a more senior conceptual engineer. When you have gone deeper into this Model of Colours you may see new angles on how to explore this whole area of selection and assessment for jobs.

Some people open out their mental Processes by adopting a new leisure pursuit, so that in a relaxed atmosphere they can 'play' with their minds in a new way. They consider this a safe way of developing themselves, since to expose less-used mental muscles to the fierce light of business thrust and parry is too risky for them. This could be a wise course. At their own pace they can exercise and develop their skills.

One woman decided that she wanted to expand the range of her thinking within the context of her family. She was a strong Blue and Red person and wanted to extend her Green. So she decided that whenever there were planning sessions amongst the family, she would let go her normal 'responsible' Red and Blue role of thinking about how to make things happen effectively. She would opt to be more Green. She deliberately threw in ideas and suggestions for alternatives, enjoying the fun of being 'irresponsible' by not putting her energy into the pragmatic part of the planning activity.

In time, as she 'practised' having ideas, she found she had them more abundantly. This started to filter into her way of working in the office and, to the surprise of her colleagues, she began to be seen as the one with the bright ideas rather than the dogsbody who could always be relied upon to get the job done well. This actually led to her promotion. By extending her range of thinking Process she became more valuable for other work which required an effective Green Process. She made a gain in personal development, job satisfaction and financial reward.

SOME QUESTIONS ARISING

* How do people's driving Colours limit and enhance their effectiveness – in work, in the home, in relationships?

* How can those limits, when they are negative, be turned to good use rather than constraining effectiveness?

* Is it a good or bad thing to have a driving force?

* What implications are there for matching the driving force of a job with the driving force of an individual's thinking style?

* How can you set about extending your range of use of the Colours through training, awareness, self-development, job rotation, leisure activities and so on?

* Are there any ways in which to identify quickly which tasks require which kind of driving force?

* Can the driving force of different people be identified without using an assessment method or test?

* Can the driving force of a leisure pursuit be identified in any way?

* Is there a good way for putting together groups of people so that their driving forces complement one another's for the task to be done?

We hope you will discover at least some of the answers after reading this book.

DO YOU UNDERSTAND THE COLOURS?

So far we have been looking at the meaning of the code, describing what the Colours stand for and how they differ from one another. In a rule-of-thumb way you now have a language which covers every aspect of your thinking.

Let's just put to the test the notion that all your thinking is covered in the Three Colours. Here is a list of sentences that anyone might use in ordinary conversation. See if you can place each one of them within one or other of the Colours. Just tick the column you think each sentence belongs in.

B	R	G	
			1. 'How are you getting on?'
			2. 'Did you say that you would be coming?'
			3. 'This is exactly what happened.'
			4. 'I just don't believe you.'
			5. 'Do buy it – it suits you so well.'
			6. 'Why don't we try by writing to Jim?'
			7. 'What if the girls turn up late?'
			8. 'Maybe you should go as "The Invisible Man!"'
			9. 'Can't you please try to get to the fair, for my sake?'
			10. 'Don't tell me, you've made a mistake!'
			11. 'I was hoping to get away by now!'
			12. 'Just like you to drop this on me at the last minute.'
			13. 'Wouldn't it be possible to patch it with Sellotape?'

Did you find that you could place some sentences in more than one column? Mark the alternatives with a question mark. Were there any you couldn't place? Here is one allocation of the sentences:

1. Red	2. Red	3. Red	4. Blue
5. Blue	6. Green	7. Green	8. Green
9. Blue	10. Blue	11. Red	12. Blue
13. Green			

This allocation is based on being sure about the intention that lies behind each of the sentences. But in conversational speech, indeed in all language, it is always difficult to be sure of the intention of the speaker or writer. Usually we deduce intention from the context, or the tone of voice, or even the punctuation, when it's written speech. But we often get that wrong. The Colours provide a means of checking someone's intention, especially as they cause you to question it.

Take sentence 13, 'Wouldn't it be possible to patch it with Sellotape?' If the speaker has a Green intention, then he is reaching for a new idea to which he is as yet uncommitted, but in which he sees a possibility of solving the problem. But it could be a Blue intention that is driving the speaker. His meaning then is, 'In my judgement it can be patched with Sellotape so let's get on and do it.' In Green the speaker is offering a suggestion, in Blue he is committing himself to doing it because he has made a judgement that it will work.

The difference between these two intentions leads to different action. In Green the speaker is quite willing to spend time exploring other ideas, but in Blue he is probably impatient to get on with it. If you take the wrong meaning, thinking he is in Green when he is really in Blue, you might cause him extreme irritation by going into Green yourself and throwing out all sorts of other ways in which to mend whatever needs patching. Indeed, if you are the sort who leads with your Green (as shown by your Chart) then it is quite likely that you will do just that.

Just imagine the conversation, if he says to you in Blue:

'Wouldn't it be possible to patch it with Sellotape?' and you respond in Green with:

'I'd like to try masking-tape, or Elastoplast. Maybe glue. Blu-tak. Spittle might do it. Or Cow-gum.'

'Stop!' he'd cry, just as you were getting into your stride with alternative ideas pouring out of you. 'I just want to get this done quickly. I've got some Sellotape right here in my pocket so let's just get on with it.'

You might retaliate in Blue: 'Sellotape is *not* the best way to do it. We ought to consider how secure we need the patch to be.'

'I've already done that,' he snaps, 'and Sellotape will do very nicely.'

'Well,' you say, still smarting from his quashing of your ideas, 'I don't agree.'

And you are into a silly little argument. Had you appreciated one another's starting points in different Colours you could have avoided this hassle. How might the conversation have gone, had you both appreciated one another's intentions?

So he begins, 'Wouldn't it be possible to patch it with Sellotape?'

Uncertain whether he is in Blue or Green, you say, 'Does it have to be Sellotape or was that just a suggestion?'

If he is in Green he is likely to respond, 'Oh, just an idea I thought might work. Do you have any others?' This signals you to go into Green too, where your suggestions will be welcomed.

If he is in Blue he is likely to respond, 'It seems a quick and easy method to get this repaired so we can get on with things' – which signals to you that he is in Blue, that he has made a judgement about the way he reckons he can get the job done effectively, so you had better be sensitive if you want to introduce other ideas.

Incidentally, a Red response to his question about using Sellotape could have gone like this: 'Well, the break-point of Sellotape is several pounds, and the glue is claimed to last three years before drying out. It won't shrink perceptibly and it's waterproof on its outside – but comes off in no time if the material itself gets wet.'

This is intended to be raw, objective information, that might be useful in deciding how to patch the thing. Such information is usually based on guesses at what really matters in the choice: for instance, durability is irrelevant if you only want the fix to hold for a few seconds. Then spittle might be very handy.

It is significant that you can interpret this one insignificant sentence about patching with Sellotape in three different ways, often through your own leading Colour. This is also true of all the other sentences, and indeed most sentences we meet in everyday life. It is a real part of the problem of communication. But by skilful use of the Colours, you can sharpen your listening skills to detect the intention underlying the words that people utter. We all know that 'it's not what you say, it's the way that you say it!'

CHAPTER THREE

Bias Between the Modes

Each Colour can be used in one or other of two Modes. Which one you adopt when using a particular Colour makes a profound difference to the outcome, because they each operate in opposing ways. If you are not aware of these dynamics between the two Modes, you will be less able to get the best out of them. But when you handle them well, harmonizing the potential conflict, they help you to match up to the realistic complexities of life. We have called the two Modes 'Hard' and 'Soft', though as with the Colours themselves these words are metaphorical and not literal in their meaning.

Most people operate with a bias towards either Hard or Soft. 'Bias' is a word used in the ancient game of Bowls. Each bowl (ball) is specially shaped and weighted on one side with lead, which makes it always veer in that direction. When aiming their bowl along the lawn at the target the player must be aware of this tendency to veer to left or right; their skill is to take the most advantage of it in their approach. Bias therefore seemed an especially appropriate word to describe one's tendency to either a Hard or a Soft approach.

Just as you were able to make a Chart of your Three Colours in the previous Chapter, you can now make Scales showing your own bias. The Scales here are specially designed for the book so that you can do it yourself. As with the Chart, you are required to make choices about the types of thinking that you prefer, and you need to follow the same rules as you did for completing the Chart in Chapter Two.

Making Your Modal Scales

A series of paired statements are presented here to give you choices between the Modes. With each pair, ask yourself which of the two statements you prefer and show your preferences with a distribution of 10 between them. Take the same approach as you did with the Colour Chart, except that here you are striking the balance between only two alternatives each time.

Some examples of how you might score:

> *If you like one statement to the complete exclusion of the other:* 10 and 0

> *If you like one statement slightly better than the other:* 6 and 4

> *If you prefer one statement a lot more than the other:* 7 and 3

Try your hand at scoring between the pairs of statements that follow. Remember that if you want to get useful Scales you must do them all.

THE MODES OF BLUE

When I have to come to a judgement on something:

Score

A I make sure I am making valid comparisons.	. . .
B I am often ready to go out on a limb and estimate, even if roughly, how things will happen in the future.	. . .
C What matters to me is what matters to me! Judgement has to be driven by what I feel and value, whether these are long-held personal values or immediate objectives or criteria for the task in hand.	. . .
D I go for the nub of the situation, fastening on any patterns to be found in its complexity or diversity.	. . .
E I try to interpret the available information by putting it together my way, so as to draw out the connections and relationships most useful to me.	. . .
F If I see things that seem similar, I have to discover what's significant about this, regardless of whether it suits me personally.	. . .

G   I often feel the need to hold off before committing myself to action so that I can ensure that things have been thought through in a sound way. . . .

H   I will try to force the thing along – no use being in doubt about everything. . . .

THE MODES OF RED

When the need is for information that will reflect reality:

J   I do a lot of finding out without recording the details, preferring to absorb impressions that will really indicate what the situation is. . . .

K   My method is to get facts and figures that are as accurate and specific as possible. . . .

L   Until you know the scale of the issue, it is impossible to sort out the best way to tell what you know and what you don't. . . .

M   I put data of a similar kind together. This also dictates my approach for investigation and the kind of questions to ask. . . .

N It's easy to get only half the picture. If I really want to know I make sure I look for what surrounds the situation and for what is hidden within it too.	. . .
P I trust in my senses, what I see and hear, feel and smell – that tells me what is what. My own camera doesn't lie.	. . .

Q I insist on data that can be properly quantified.	. . .
R You cannot ignore things you notice just because they cannot be measured and clearly identified.	. . .

THE MODES OF GREEN

When the situation cries out for new ideas:

S The secret is to allow your mind to bring out something new through the pictures and images that form if you encourage them. For me, that's what imagination means.	. . .
T I will readily challenge the need to conform and will break the mould with alacrity.	. . .

U   I just go on Sixth Sense.

. . .

V   The way to real ideas is to start from what already exists in some tangible shape or form – and then keep on changing various aspects of it. By exploring many possibilities you are sure to reach something new that's better.

. . .

W   I take positive delight in being ingenious – fooling the system without actually cheating.

. . .

X   My way is to imagine that things are quite different and then throw up many scenarios as if they could be really true.

. . .

Y   I keep trying to find more exceptions to what I saw at first.

. . .

Z   What helps me is to keep open and flexible as long as possible. This lets in new ideas.

. . .

YOUR COLOUR MODES

Count up your scores as shown below and put them into the boxes.

BLUE		RED		GREEN	
A+D	B+C	K+M	J+L	T+V	S+U
+F+G	+E+H	+N+Q	+P+R	+W+Y	+X+Z
Hard	Soft	Hard	Soft	Hard	Soft

You might get more out of the bald figures above by making a visual display of them.

Display these scores spatially, using the Scales in Figure 3.1. The Scales become a reference that is easy to understand and remember, especially when you take care to fill them in accurately and attractively. Using Colour pencils or felt pens, Blue, Red and Green, make your own Colour Mode Scales with your Hard and Soft scores. Be sure you work from the central zero line outwards to left and right. (See examples on the following pages.) If you want to make the Scales easy to read, you could Colour the Hards and the Softs with different, distinctive patterns.

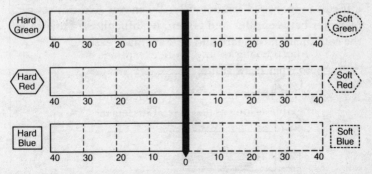

3.1

The strength of your Bias towards either Soft or Hard is made obvious by the Scales. For a quick interpretation of your Colour Modes, there is a variety of examples below, with short explanations of the significance of their different scores. Find the one that most closely resembles yours overall.

Interpreting Your Colour Mode Scales

THE NATURE OF BIAS

1. If your bias shows as being either all towards Soft or all towards Hard in all the Colours (Figure 3.2), you are so consistently lop-sided that you may actually be able to manage quite well. Others will have to get used to making allowances; it'll certainly be necessary, for lack of the opposite Modes may seriously handicap your effectiveness.

3.2 Stark examples of bias

2. If your bias shows with two Colours towards Soft and one towards Hard, or vice versa (Figure 3.3) your thinking is more difficult to manage harmoniously. Whenever Red can act as a mediator between Blue and Green the difficulties of managing the combinations of Hard and Soft are made easier.

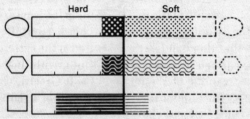

3.3 Variegated extremes

3. A fairly even balance between the Hard and Soft in any Colour may not be so ideal as you might imagine. Oddly enough, this lack of Bias may produce an awkward dissonance between the Hard and Soft, especially if combined with a High Score in that Colour. In Figure 3.4 we show just one of the many possible combinations.

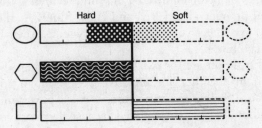

3.4 Balance or dissonance

These examples of Colour Modes only give a brief indication of the complex effects of Bias on your thinking style. When you combine Bias with your Colour Scores, you will reflect more of the richness in your pattern of thinking (see Chapter Four).

THE TWO CULTURES

The Hard and Soft Modes are often taken to typify the divided cultures of 'science' (Hard) and 'art' (Soft). Typical caricatures of scientists depict them in the extremes of the Hard Mode: for example, the astronomer measuring the distance to the sun from Mars to the last millionth of a millimetre (Hard Red) who never sees the beauty of the moon dappling the leaves of the tree through the window and across his desk (Soft Red). Arts people, on the other hand, are caricatured at the extremes of the Soft Mode, driven by passion (Soft Blue), with their heads in the clouds dreaming of Wonderland (Soft Green), while their business goes bust under their feet for want of attention to the accounts (Hard Red and Hard Blue).

This setting apart of the Modes into two warring camps does

no justice to the reality of how people actually make use of their Hard and Soft. Einstein is reputed to have conceived the idea of relativity while dreamily watching dust dancing in sunbeams (Soft Green). By using Hard Red and Blue he was then able to verify his hypothesis. The Disney wonderlands are made magic (through Soft Red and Soft Green) and made available to Everyman by being embedded in sound technology and tough financial practice (Hard Red and Hard Blue). At the highest levels of excellence you will see people who use their Hard and Soft in symbiosis.

Hard and Soft are the two sides to our thinking which must be brought together for effective action in all spheres of endeavour. Sadly, the caricatures have a powerful hold on imagination. Scientists are feared because they are perceived to embody only the virtues of Hard thinking. Businessmen and managers are tarred with the same brush, because they exhibit so clearly the Hard. They are accused of lacking the 'human' side of thinking, of operating with machine-like minds, and basing their actions only on cold Hard logic. On the other hand, painters, actors, musicians, dancers, fashion-makers, are often not taken seriously in society at large because they are seen to reflect only the wonder of Soft thinking. They are accused of avoiding reality, of being too dedicated to their art and living their lives out of high-flown ideals.

As this book unravels more about the natures of the Hard and Soft Modes of all the Colours, the aim is to give you access to every corner, every nook and cranny of your thinking, so that you can go beyond these caricatures. We all need to be both scientist and artist. We have to live in the Hard world of objective reality and we also have to live in the Soft inner world of our own beliefs, dreams and values. These two have to be brought together for a sane society to be built, where art and science enjoy mutual respect, learn from each other and recognize that the thinking skills the other uses are relevant, and indeed essential for the vitality, enrichment and evolution of both. All good scientists are artists. All good artists are scientists.

The earlier Model of Three Colours could now be seen no

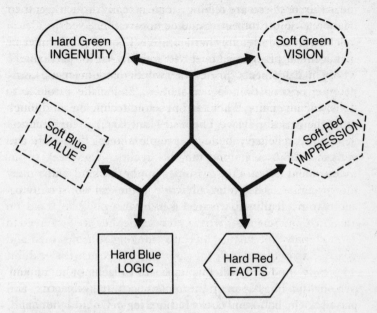

3.5 The six directions

longer as a simple tripod, but one whose main limbs each fork
out into two branches, one Hard and the other Soft. Now there
are six directions in your thinking to take into account (Figure
3.5). This chapter will explain these six with increasing depth.

THE HARD MODE

All the Hard Modes reveal the kind of thinking that focuses *out*
into the world, that directs attention towards the tangible
realities of things. It is 'objective', in that it attempts to remove
the subjectiveness of personal feelings, views, opinions, means
of expression, intuition, hunches, guesses, and so on. When
you are using the Hard Modes, your intentions are solidly
grounded in a tangible kind of reality. It doesn't matter whether
you are giving or finding out information (Red), or making or
influencing judgements (Blue), or generating or receiving new

ideas (Green); you are relying on an approach which seems to be more absolute, objective and demonstrable.

The Hard Modes are 'hard nosed'. They are enshrined in management practice all over the Western world, particularly where managements pride themselves on efficiency, competence, organization, logical analysis, financial controls, systems, and ingenuity. They can be seen as driving the disciplines of mathematics, physics, chemistry, accounting, engineering, geography, geology, biology, programming. These are the subjects which rely upon tangible reality. They seek to be independent from the personal, to be beyond individual interpretation. They must all 'work' in the real world of living and man-made things, whoever is using them.

THE SOFT MODE

The Soft Modes reveal the inner dimensions of mind and personality. They open up the unconscious, the subjective, the personal, the half-known, the fathomless well of individuality. When you are using your Soft Modes your intentions are to express your values and your beliefs (Blue), to reveal your hidden imagination (Green), or to capture the implicit truth (Red) which lies within and around the explicit reality.

The Soft Modes drive activities such as politics, diplomacy, communication, broadcasting, selling, marketing, education, personnel and advertising. Like the performing arts and fine arts, they are seen as difficult to quantify and therefore somehow more qualitative. These Modes work on the hearts and minds of people, to influence their attitudes, their ways of perceiving the world and themselves. The acceptance and good use of the Soft Modes are dependent upon unspoken and unmeasurable confidence and trust between people. They work best when the personal is brought to bear, and when individuals are prepared to invest their own intuition, insight and 'human' interpretation.

THE EFFECT OF HARD AND SOFT IN EACH COLOUR

Within each of the Colours the Mode either of Hard or of Soft takes on particular characteristics. So the qualities of Hard Red are different from Hard Blue and yet again from Hard Green. Similarly for Soft in each Colour. The fundamental nature of Hard, as the objective, outward-looking, tangible Mode, and that of Soft as the subjective, inward-looking, intangible Mode, applies throughout all the Colours. But individual Colours cause the Hard and Soft to be expressed in different ways.

THE BLUE MODES

It is the nature of all Blue thinking to form an opinion in order to decide upon something. Blue is used when Red information is not complete. Judgement simply has to be brought to bear when the full truth (Red) actually is not known. It is then that you must decide (Blue) what is best to do, based on the perhaps inadequate information that you have.

A prime example of this is the jury's decision-making in a court of law. How that jury form their opinions will depend on the balance between the Hard and Soft Blue in the make-up of the members. They can come to their decision of guilty or not guilty by two routes – through the Hard route or the Soft.

Hard Blue This mode of thinking is characterized by clear reasoning. We typically describe this as rational thought and most academics would consider Hard Blue, what they would call intellectual rigour, to be a major tool in their mental kit-bags. A decision made in Hard Blue is reached by sound, logical steps which can be tested for their validity with objective deductions from whatever solid evidence (Hard Red) is available.

When you make use of your Hard Blue thinking, you bring to bear relevant and reasoned arguments on an issue. You endeavour to establish an objective case upon which to form an opinion that attempts to be as personally unbiased as possible.

If you were in the dock you would probably hope it would be this impartial Mode that would dominate when a jury sought to reach a verdict. Unless, of course, you were guilty, when you could only hope the jury would be 'on your side' or feel terrified lest they were prejudiced against you (Soft Blue).

Soft Blue In complete contrast to Hard Blue, the strength of Soft Blue lies in its dependence on personal interpretation to arrive at a conclusion. The inner integrity of individual values is what counts here. The quality of this Mode in Blue is perhaps most strongly represented by the phrase 'I want'. You can see this even in babies. Whether it is fuelled by instinctual drives, by basic physical emotions, by values and beliefs affected by our upbringing and society, or by sheer individual aspirations, Soft Blue determines what *you* aim for, what is ideal for *you*. When we seek to do the right thing from our Soft Blue we do it on the basis of whether we 'like' or 'dislike', whether we 'want' or 'don't want', possibly regardless of the logic of the case.

To return to our jury. If a majority of members rely on their Soft Blue to guide their judgement, then their personal likes and dislikes towards the prisoner in the dock will sway their decision, regardless of any logical reasoning. How often a judge warns the jury not to be influenced by their distaste for the crime and their desire to pin the guilt on someone who may look suspicious to them. He urges them to use their Hard Blue on the Hard Red evidence before the court to reach their judgement. Sometimes he urges in vain, for the power of Soft Blue can persuade a jury to convict, whatever reasoning might indicate to the contrary.

Soft Blue reflects how things are valued. It is the energy that drives you, how you direct your actions, what you aim for, your motive, intentions, and criteria. However hard we may try to be objective, we cannot avoid interpreting what we see through our own personally tinted lenses. When we make predictions, they are so easily affected by what we wish for, what we expect and want to believe. The side you take on any issue is strongly influenced when your Soft Blue is operating. This is the Mode of persuasion, of negotiation and selling and agreeing, of likes and dislikes and personal taste. Issues that are emotive draw on and inflame the Soft Blue area of the mind. Politics, religion, morals, divorce, race and class relations, money – anything that arouses passion, anger, zeal, ardour, fear, courage, and suchlike emotions is the stuff of Soft Blue.

Soft Blue is exciting, excited, warm. And just because it is the natural and spontaneous side of our human judgement it has a power that requires the discipline of Hard Blue reason. When you balance the two sides of your judgement, it seems like wisdom.

Hard and Soft Compared The good use of judgement holds the balance between the Hard Blue of reason and the Soft Blue of reasons. It provides a hard structure or framework of sound logic, so that the strong Soft forces of human energy can be firmly anchored and contained. Of course, for good decision-making we should call upon both Modes of Blue to ensure the appropriate balance of reason (Hard) and emotion (Soft). It would be a very narrow view of judgement that confined it to a court of law. Yet such is the power of connotations that the word 'judge' summons up awesome pictures of power, severity and fear – although judges are as likely to be humble, benign and humorous. To convey the meanings, the metaphor 'Blue' really is more useful than the proper word 'Judge'.

Left to themselves, Blue energies can work in an undisciplined way that is often disastrous. For instance, it's easy to make comparisons between things that are not legitimately comparable in the context of the situation. In Hard Blue, like should be compared with like.

So, in making a case for a wages claim, is it legitimate to compare the wages of steel workers in two different countries simply using the exchange rate to translate guilders, lira or francs into pounds? A more logical and less value-laden comparison might be based on how long it takes in the different countries to earn a loaf or a bottle of wine or a washing machine – and then, how comparable are these?

We all jump to conclusions at the drop of a hat, driven by Soft Blue to interpret everything we see from our own personal viewpoint. These 'instinctive' guesses and flashes of prediction need testing with the Hard Blue discipline of reason.

For instance, if you say smoking is the cause of cancer, how do you account for Mary's cancer, when she has never smoked in her life? At first sight, this test of logic seems to annihilate the conclusion reached. But even further rigour could be applied. By focusing hard on exactly what is enclosed within the word 'smoking', you could say that without ever having a cigarette between her lips, Mary has ingested huge quantities of smoke over long periods because she has always worked in a pub.

Such are the roles played by Hard Blue. It is more than interesting to watch the interplay between Hard and Soft when we are taken up by some real-life drama. It always highlights the critical role of thinking when we look in the newspapers and see how humanity responds when the chips are down.

THE RED MODES

Without information, your power is emasculated. When in Red you are driving for truth, for non-judgemental, dispassionate reality. Red thinking is aware of what 'is' and what 'has been'. It is open to receiving any information that throws light on truth. But truth, as we know, has many faces. We need the two Modes of Red in order to be able to detect all of them. Hard Red alone sees only one kind of truth. Soft Red sees another. Both are important. If either is neglected the whole truth is imperilled by one-sidedness. It is indeed chastening to reflect that in our court of law, the judge is obliged to instruct the jury not to take any notice of certain kinds of evidence when they are not seen as legitimately Hard.

Hard Red This kind of thinking collects data in details, in items, in pieces, in minutiae, in facts, in specifics. Item by item it accumulates bits of information which are then allocated to suitable categories for coherence and completeness of reference. Because so much work is involved, mankind through the centuries has developed many kinds of instrument to help him do it, the latest being our friendly computer.

Hard Red thinking enables us to 'get hold of' our world, to measure it, to contain it, to know it in its material details and so manage it into segments of knowledge. What happened in the past is stored as history, archaeology, geology. What constitutes the world today is sociology, politics, zoology, psychology, physics, chemistry, botany. Hard Red seeks to describe everything. Through it we are able to master our environment and to know about ourselves.

In olden days, and even now in certain societies, knowledge was stored in human memory and passed on from generation to generation by word of mouth alone. Capturing this knowledge, including for example old folk songs and poetry, in written form has made it more reliably and enduringly available. Indeed, the wealth of human knowledge is contained in the reference libraries of the world. Today, with the increasing sophistication of computers, this wealth is recognized as the most precious commodity we have to trade with one another. Information Technology has been born. As yet it still deals almost exclusively in Hard Red.

Hard Red often requires laborious effort, the painstaking accumulation of information, over months and years. It requires patience to gather its fruits. The verification of scientific hypotheses rests on dependable Hard Red thinking. Darwin toiled for years on his voyages to collect and record the information which fuelled his mind. While his Blue and Green thinking was involved to create his imaginative ideas on evolution, his long years of work in Hard Red were the seed-bed.

Soft Red Soft Red captures and conveys the spirit of truth, the implicit reality, rather than the explicit. Soft Red can offer an immediate grasp of truth, capturing in an instant the essence of an atmosphere, a place, a scene, a person, an attitude, a stance, a manner, a pose. Soft Red often sees a whole in a moment of perception. It reveals the qualitative rather than the quantitative. This is truth on a different level from the accuracy of the Hard Red, but just as necessary. Indeed, the art of conveying this kind of truth commands fees and even status that positions some exponents near the top of their community.

Returning to our court room, great defence lawyers such as Rufus Isaacs or F E Smith have always made ready use of Soft Red. Supreme artists in the medium of communication, they see clearly that the impressions conveyed can be even more important than what is actually said and recorded. The theory behind adversarial advocacy is that from the dialectics of two opposing sides, truth will triumph in the end.

A delicate line can separate the choosing of impressions that will convey truth (Soft Red), and the creation of a favourable impression, one that will influence or bend someone's judgement along the lines you want (Soft Blue). Impressing someone is more likely to be Soft Blue than Red. And this may indicate how useful the Colour code can be, compared with 'plain language'.

'The pen is mightier than the sword.' The writers of the world have moved it more profoundly and often more enduringly than great generals, politicians or captains of industry. Of course, some famous wielders of the sword were able to write or speak marvellously as well. Then see what happens, especially when all the best tunes are given to the devil – a Robespierre of the French Revolution, or Adolph Hitler, say. The verdict of history might well be that the oratory of Winston Churchill contributed more to his beleaguered island's survival than his conduct of the war.

Hard and Soft Compared At a more homely level, it is by Soft Red thinking that we can understand the real or underlying message of a poem, or a story, or a symphony. We can 'know' another person at a first meeting through our Soft Red. It enables us to appreciate what is implicit in a situation – so we can avoid putting both feet in it. We all rely upon our Soft Red a great deal to get through every day. For as we talk with colleagues, friends, family, we expect them to absorb the nub, the essence of what we say, without having to spell out every last detail. And they rely upon us to do the same. So when you are faced with someone who does not use their Soft Red, conversation, communication, is stymied, until you get the drift of how to switch into Hard Red specifics. You find yourself having to state things in ways you would never have thought necessary. And if you are describing anything in writing to them, it is actually counter-productive to express ideas in a variety of ways. The Hard Red approach of the accountant, the engineer or the technical expert is to value consistency of labelling much more than analogy.

Bringing verbal agreements into a paper contract has a similar effect. As the company lawyer of a Dutch organization said to us apologetically but with subtle humour, 'Well, now we must reduce our agreement into writing.' He knew that 'reducing' the agreement (Soft) to 'writing' (Hard) might by exactitude destroy the flavour of an agreement that had been reached through informal conversation and practice.

It is indeed difficult to capture the spirit of an agreement (Soft) in the letter of the law (Hard). And who is to say which is really the more important?

You may notice that three- to six-year-olds lack Soft Red: they love the details of Hard Red. Conversation with children of these ages is filled with numbers, lists, and with attention to factual accuracy (Hard Red). So you may say jocularly to your four-year-old, 'How's that dear old Teddy of yours?' The message of affection that was intended within your question might be completely missed by your child. 'My Teddy isn't old,' she replies. 'He's two next week. He's not as old as me. My Teddy's a young Teddy.'

A Soft Red intention has misfired! You chose to code your remark intending to suit your child's understanding, but she hears your affectionate 'old' as a statement of chronology. Young children do take things very, very literally (Hard Red).

Soft Red is either hidden within, or found in the whole which is greater than the sum of the parts. When it is hidden within it is like a poem where the message is never specifically stated but intrinsic in it.

> *Do not smile to yourself*
> *Like a green mountain*
> *With a cloud drifting across it.*
> *People will know we are in love.*

– Lady Otomo No Sakanoe: Eighth Century, Japan.

When Soft Red is to be found in the whole it is like an impressionist painting. If you look at the brush strokes, at the daubs and splashes, at the Hard Red details, then you will fail to see the field ready for harvest and the sweep of the wind through the corn. Whistler, the painter, one day rebuked a woman who was peering up close to one of his paintings: 'Madam, paintings are made to be looked at, not smelt.'

When Hard and Soft Red look at the same situation at the same time they see it differently. If they are not careful they may ignore one another's perceptions. But it is the difference that brings the richness to the grasp of truth, as well as knowing when each Mode is appropriate. Hard and Soft need to dialogue with each other to discover 'the Truth, the whole Truth'.

THE GREEN MODES

The search for ideas leads thinking into the unknown. Green thinkers turn ever to the future, to what might be. Most education systems neglect the development of this kind of thinking beyond the first stages of schooling. Play and fantasy are often thought fit only for children; they are firmly squashed in teenagers, who are channelled into knowing and understanding only what is already known. Like Blue and Red, Green has its two Modes which reveal very different approaches to realizing what is new.

Hard Green This thinking is fertile in making connections, in networking, to form new possibilities out of existing circumstances. Hard Green seeks originality through being ingenious. It twists and turns, darting in different directions, exploring hither and thither, in and out, up and down, round and about, all with the intention of generating yet another way of reaching a goal. If there is a problem blocking the path, then the Hard Green mind will search around, throwing up options in abundance. It is associated with fluency, not in words so much as ideas.

Hard Green directly challenges 'what has always been', by questioning the usefulness of habits. It turns custom upside-down, is no respecter of persons, seeing every institutionalized procedure as fair game. Hard Green, by flouting convention brings hope of change into fixed, static, constipated organizations and systems. Hard Green also gets around difficulties, being a kind of lateral thinking. Where Hard Blue would wrestle logically with a problem, or Hard Red would collect information in order to understand the problem better, Hard Green jumps outside it, takes up a totally different perspective and thus 'escapes' from the problem. When a chosen course of action seems likely to produce adverse as well as positive results, Hard Green will look for ways out of the adverse while retaining the positive. Recycling of used goods is an example of this, avoiding waste-disposal costs and creating additional resources from 'spent' products.

Until quite recently, those who mined gravel by gouging out great pits in the ground were obliged by law to fill them up again, and would often make use of the space for refuse disposal. Nowadays, they are just as likely to allow the pits to fill with water, making beautiful lakes and bird sanctuaries, places for refreshment of the soul and a wide variety of leisure pursuits. Done well, this is a high value-added alternative to creating hideous dumps. It is commercially as well as environmentally desirable.

What about more ingenious disposal of our rubbish? That's still a problem to exercise our Green. In Holland, where the land is extremely flat, artificial hills have been created and landscaped. In Florida, mountains of car tyres have been placed on the sea bed for sand to gather round, providing a much-needed habitat for certain kinds of sea life. There are hundreds of possibilities waiting to be found. Including perhaps a harder look at the various stages in the very creation of rubbish itself, right back to the original design of the product and its packaging by the manufacturer.

Most of the ideas you get come through Hard Green. You are using it all the time whenever you try to do something better. Look around the shops, or even your place of work. Most of the products you see have been invented by changing, modifying or improving something that already existed. Give a Hard Green mind something to start with and it will generate all sorts of permutations and variations of the original. This is how to get many ideas, some of which will be truly unusual and offer an ingenious solution to a problem. We are even beginning to harness computers in Hard Green to speed up the generation of ideas. The process, known 'in the trade' as morphology, combines and permutates variations of factors and was in use before we had computers.

Soft Green This kind of thinking reaches out far beyond Hard Green to discover new ideas. It finds its source in pictures, images and dreams. It is 'other-worldly', or beyond this world. Soft Green thinking is inspired by glimpses of feelings that stretch forward into the future. Imagination is at the centre of Soft Green. Being so 'way out' it can be too far ahead to be appreciated by most people.

Soft Green depends on intuition for its leads. The sixth sense is Soft Green. It can warn about and it can encourage a new venture, with confidence in its intuitive insight into the outcome. Some people rely upon their intuition, often successfully, for many of the biggest decisions in life – the house they buy, the person they marry, the career they adopt – rather than working things out logically. This intuition is also found in entrepreneurial flair, and can often look like taking risks of a high order. As Pasteur said (was it helplessly or enigmatically?): 'The trouble with imagination is that it is sometimes right.'

People in Soft Green talk of being 'in touch' with something bigger than themselves, of receiving ideas not of their own making, but 'given'. They are willing to be open minded, receptive, prayerful, meditative, contemplative, so that Mind, Intelligence, Energy, Spirit, God may enter and inspire real creativeness.

This Colour still has the liveliness of childhood fantasy, or mental play, which enables it literally to make pictures in the mind which feed the creative imagination (creatively). Pictures are so free-forming, so colourful, so flexible, so un-fixed, that they give to thinking a medium of activity which allows a wonderful richness of ideas to emerge. Image-making in the mind is conscious dreaming, allowing access to the treasures of the unconscious which can bring forth outstanding or at least unusual ideas.

Some people feel that creativity can only be Soft Green. Their concept of creativity is surrounded by an aura of genius, or unexplainable flair. ('If it can be explained, it cannot be truly creative.') They go in awe of sudden inspiration, shafts of light from heaven, as if a truly creative idea were the product of some mystical force or magic. Soft Green is working when an idea appears that is revolutionary rather than evolutionary – a quantum leap of such breathtaking scale that it transports us into a new dimension altogether.

Hard and Soft Compared To come down to earth a bit, you can see that the difference between Hard and Soft Green is akin to the difference between seeing something anew and seeing a new thing altogether. In the nature of things, we all use both, Hard Green more frequently perhaps without recognizing it, whereas Soft Green seems to make the eye gleam and the blood rush with delight and even ecstasy. At the moment of conception an idea seems to light the whole world with its brilliance. It remains to be seen how brilliant the idea really turns out to be, and for this you need Red and Blue.

CHAPTER FOUR

Interpreting Your Thinking Style

Now that you have found out about the Colours and the Modes, they will be drawn together so you can interpret the chief characteristics of your own thinking style.

As a reminder, write your scores from the questionnaires in the boxes below so you can quickly turn to them for reference as you work your way through this chapter.

Your Colours

Insert scores from Chapter Two page 34

BLUE   RED   GREEN

☐ ☐   ☐ ☐   ☐ ☐

High is 65 and above
Mid is 41 to 64 inclusive
Low is 40 and below

Underline the categories you fall into:

BLUE	RED	GREEN
High	High	High
Mid	Mid	Mid
Low	Low	Low

Your Modes

Insert scores from Chapter Three page 63

BLUE		RED		GREEN	
HARD	SOFT	HARD	SOFT	HARD	SOFT

For the purposes of interpretation, a score over 24 shows a significant bias *towards* that Mode and *away from* its opposite.

There are just a few key questions that need answering to grasp the essentials about your scores:

1. What is your leading Colour?
   What are you biased towards? (Hard or Soft?)
2. What is your lowest Colour?
   What are you biased away from? (Hard or Soft?)
3. Overall bias? (Hard or Soft?)

EXAMPLE A: ANNE

High Blue 80		Mid Red 54		Low Green 26	
HARD	SOFT	HARD	SOFT	HARD	SOFT
29	11	27	13	25	15

1. Leading Colour is Blue.
   Bias to Hard Blue from Soft.
2. Lowest Colour is Green.
   Bias away from Soft to Hard, i.e. under-uses Soft.
3. Overall Bias towards Hard (81; Soft 39).

Anne's Hard Blue is obviously the strongest feature of her style and Soft Green the weakest. We might say that she 'leads with her Hard Blue'. As she is more Hard than Soft overall, we might say she's 'a Hard thinker'. Given that her Mid Red has a noticeably Hard Bias we might also say she's 'a Hard Blue, Hard Red type'. In this shorthand way we characterize the significant features of her thinking style.

EXAMPLE B: BRIAN

Mid Blue 48		Mid Red 46		High Green 66	
HARD 19	SOFT 21	HARD 16	SOFT 24	HARD 6	SOFT 34

1. Leading Colour is Green.
   Bias towards Soft.
2. Does not have a significant Lowest Colour.
   Bias in both his secondary Colours is away from Hard although not dramatically. Under-uses Hard.
3. Overall Bias Soft (79; Hard 41).

What is important here is that the Soft Green stands out as the significant Colour in Brian's profile. One suspects that it plays a dominant role in his thinking. Brian is 'a Soft thinker'.

EXAMPLE C: CATHERINE

Mid Blue 52		Mid Red 58		Mid Green 50	
HARD 33	SOFT 7	HARD 12	SOFT 28	HARD 29	SOFT 11

1. Leading Colour is Red, but only just.
   Bias towards Soft.

2. Does not have a significant Lowest Colour.
   Bias in both her secondary Colours is markedly away from
   Soft. Under-uses Soft.
3. Overall Bias towards Hard (74; Soft 46).

Catherine's scores require some unravelling, since all her
Colours seem to be nearly equally favoured. She is an extreme
of a special kind: she has no marked Colour preference. When
scores are even why call it extreme? Our findings are that most
people have a noticeable preference so it becomes an extreme to
be evenly distributed in your preferences.

In overall numbers, Catherine's Bias between Hard and Soft
is very marked. But look at how she swings from Hard Blue to
Soft Red and back to Hard Green. This gives her a broad-based
thinking style but will present her with difficulties as she tries to
manage the interfaces between Hard and Soft.

CHECKING THE ACCURACY OF YOUR COLOUR SCORES

The scores from the questionnaires are only useful if they give a
real reflection of your thinking. If you have doubts about them,
consider two possibilities:

1. You did not rank your choices well enough in the questionnaires to reflect your intentions accurately. So your scores
   do not show your thinking as it really is. Try the questionnaires again. Your increased knowledge of the Colours and
   Modes could now actually improve the accuracy of your
   responses.
2. Maybe you do not know yourself as well as you think you do;
   the Colours could be revealing unrealized parts of your
   mind.

HOW TO USE THIS CHAPTER

1. You will find in the following sections an extensive but not
   exhaustive listing to interpret scores. It is intended to be
   sufficient for you to be able to compile a realistic picture of
   your mind from the descriptions which match your scores.

If you want to be fairly systematic without reading everything, here's a suggested route:

* Start with your leading Colour and your preferred Bias in it.
* Pick out the Modes you are Biased towards in your other Colours.
* Read up on your lowest Colour and on the Mode you are Biased away from. This reveals the most under-used part of your thinking.
* Try the opposites of your Colour scores, e.g. if you are High in Green read up Low Green. Exploring the opposite enriches your understanding of your own scores.
* We suggest that if mid scores do not figure in your thinking style you read them anyway so as to gain a balanced picture of each Colour.

2. Throughout the listings, key words and phrases are used to highlight what is important. They summarize core meanings so you can take them in at a glance.

3. In this book format it is necessary to catalogue the Colours separately for ease of reference. In life, of course, the Colours blend and merge in order to develop complex thoughts. Sometimes a person's thinking may be suffused by the force of one strong Colour. Some skilful thinkers almost dance with their Colours while others lumber clumsily around or get stuck in one. So interpreting from the book to real life is a big step (and is tackled in Chapter Five).

4. Every aspect of your mind, whether you have a high or low score, can be an asset – *when used appropriately*. After you have read about your thinking style in this chapter you can go on to discover more about how to turn everything you've got to good account.

Section One

The overall characteristic of Green thinking is the search for new ideas untrammelled by constraints of what is currently known (Red) or what is currently thought to be right (Blue).

MID GREEN SCORE

Someone with a Mid Green score likes to use the qualities of Green but not at the expense of the other Colours. Since one of the key attributes of Green is making new connections, the Mid Green mind is very good not only at connecting ideas but also at interconnecting within its own Colours. Green can act as a kind of circulating energy between Red and Blue, drawing them in when needed and phasing them out when finished. A Mid Green score indicates the ability to operate with Green without swamping your thinking with it.

There will be a liveliness and flexibility of ideas in a Mid Green mind, a readiness to explore the new and a willingness to open up to what might even be outlandish. Green people are unlikely to bear grudges (unless they have a strong Soft Blue component) because their lively minds are energized by an 'uncommitted commitment' to the future. Grudges only arise when people cling to the past, which Green never does.

One very important thing to appreciate about anyone who is operating in Green is that while they are actually in Green they selfishly pursue the gleam of newness to the exclusion of all else. It is the nature of Green to be absorbed in the idea. The generation of new ideas and new visions causes people to be oblivious to the niceties of manners, to the demands of the clock, or to the state of their own or others' physical needs. Meals go by the board until the Green phase passes.

> **Hard Bias in Mid Green: 'Every problem is an opportunity in disguise'**

If you have a Bias towards Hard you will probably be inclined always to try to get the most you can out of a situation, whether things are good or bad, by generating lots of alternatives. Hard Green is essentially **Ingenious**, and able by flexible and adaptable thinking to **Re-describe** problems to get out of a hole. Hard Green people **Challenge** assumptions to break out of constraints and they will persist and **Pursue** ideas, never giving up hope of finding yet another alternative that might do the job better. Theirs is a busy mind which, as soon as it takes hold of a thought, plays with it, changes it and turns it into something else.

This flexibility and mobility of thought usually produces a quick and witty sense of humour which overturns norms and reveals absurdities. Hard Green minds usually work fast, so in the overflowing abundance of connections between what is normal and what is not, some are bound to turn out to be amusing. Hard Green people often cultivate this ability and become known for their wit. Frank Muir and Denis Norden, comedy scriptwriters and beloved by fans of BBC panel games, are brilliant examples of this kind of humour developed to a very fine art: off-the-cuff and very funny. The quality that typifies this aspect of Hard Green is the ability to **Escape** from the channels of the mind, the rules of the game, the customs of behaviour, the middle-of-the-road course, into allusions and turn-abouts that defeat constraints without outraging law, rules and morality (too much, anyway). Skilful Hard Green manages that tightrope.

> **Soft Bias in Mid Green: 'A gift of the gods'**

A Bias to Soft is found in the intuitive thinker who bypasses logic (Blue) and evidence (Red) to arrive, with what sometimes seems to be unfair good luck, at ideas which in their visionary quality outshine all others. The battle between Mozart and Salieri (as the story is told in the film *Amadeus*) exemplifies this. Almost without effort the most wonderful music poured from the playful Mozart, born out of him by seemingly undeserved divine inspiration. He had an intuitive **Feel** for the sublime. Such is Soft Green's nature. Worthy Salieri, however, who worked and prayed for such gifts, only produced worthy music. How unfair! Mozart allowed his mind to remain open, **Unformed**, so that he could respond to impulses from dimensions of experience which lie outside the normal.

The Soft Green mind is rich in imagery, colour, pictures and symbols. Thinking in Soft Green is fuelled by imagination, the capacity not only to **Symbolize** reality in pictures but also to **Pretend** that you are somewhere else, or somebody else, with vivid reality. You can, in Soft Green, become anything you want, go anywhere you want, and actually 'see' yourself in your mind's eye in living images. There is increasing evidence to show that some people who excel in this Mode do 'receive' pictures which convey visions of the future with clarity and precision. The dilemma then arises of how to tell others of their visions without being labelled 'nutters'. Western society does not, as yet, understand this kind of thinking. Westerners who are educated and trained in logic (Hard Blue) and evident truth (Hard Red) do not know how to handle Soft Green, so they mistrust it and tend to ostracize anyone using it. A pity, because if they learned how to work with it they would discover many short cuts and insights to transform their ways of looking into and preparing for the future. This is an art of thinking much needed in our radically changing world.

HIGH GREEN SCORE

The amusing and tragic Greek legend of Pandora's box typifies the High Green mind at work. Forbidden to open the enchanting box, warned that it would do her no good, Pandora's curiosity (Green) overwhelmed her good sense (Blue). Her folly brought cares and woe into the world where before all was happiness and light. When Green is over-used and applied at moments when it is not relevant, the effects can be devastating. It is usually left to other people to cope with the results; having caused havoc by turning everyone else's world upside-down, the Green mind moves on to pastures new. High Green is **Uncommitted,** except to having new ideas, and more new ideas, and more. Consequences are of little concern to it.

Yet there is also something wonderfully liberating when Green is outrageous in the face of convention. People who are heavily Green just need to learn to be more timely in picking their moments for disturbing the peace. Their problem is finding the self-control to keep track of ideas when their brains are teeming with them. They fear losing the ideas if they do not get them immediately into circulation, so they can be impatient and rude. Whether the idea itself is good or not is not an issue for them. The priority is expressing the thought and giving it air-time, so that it can see the light of day and begin to grow. Unless Green meets Green when sounding off, the seeding ideas may fall on stony Blue ground and perish.

When someone has a very Green mind they often experience rejection. Ideas are so exciting to them that it can be bewildering when they are not always taken up with enthusiasm by others. Novelty fires the energy of Green thinkers. They sparkle inside. They can overwhelm Blues and Reds with the fertility of their prolific minds – and turn them off completely. 'What stupid ideas. Won't work,' say the Blues. 'How half-baked! Where's the evidence?' say the Reds. Many Green people are loners, nursing their imaginations in a hostile world because they have relied so heavily on the strength of their Green thinking without also cultivating a sense of appropriateness.

They may also be quite difficult to 'read' because their body language often does not match what they are really thinking: the signals they give off, without intending to, may have nothing to do with what's in their mind. So they can scowl or look bored or appear to be rude or seem uncaring whilst entertaining inner thoughts of quite a different nature. This can be hard to deal with until you realize they are Green.

Hard Bias in High Green: 'Never knowing when to stop'

Bias to Hard is liable to bring these kinds of drawbacks for the High Green person. You will be a disconcerting person for those who cannot stomach your uncontrolled avalanche of Green ideas. You will put slower thinkers off their stroke by the speed of your reactions to ideas. Because you like to dart around, picking up thoughts from wherever they come and sending them on reshaped but undigested, you may seldom get down to the pedestrian, but necessary steps of sorting out which ideas to develop and innovate.

These Hard High Green people may also fail to accept received wisdom as a basis for action because they feel they must challenge *everything*. This is frequently experienced by their colleagues as time-wasting and annoying; they see them as larking around instead of getting on with the job. Indeed one of the biggest traps Hard Greens fall into is violating time-limits on tasks. When colleagues urge them impatiently to get down to action they are often still pursuing the next 'marvellous' idea that has just popped into their heads.

Soft Bias in High Green: 'Beautiful dreamer, open your eyes'

Bias to Soft in High Green can lead one to become wildly unrealistic if not grounded with some steadying common-sense. If Soft Green thinkers scorn the practical things in life they can end up in Cloud-cuckoo-land and the dole queue. Flower-power hippies of the 1960s had painful lessons to learn reconciling their dreams of peace and beauty with mundane toil such as community washing-up rotas (Red).

If you are a High Soft Green, watch your tendencies to want to remain uncommitted and unformed. Notice if you repeatedly hold back from putting your positive seal on decisions, letting things go by default rather than coming down on one side or the other. Soft Greens who always appear vague extend the patience of their colleagues beyond endurance. We have all met the person who smiles sweetly and confesses, 'No, I haven't made up my mind yet, I am waiting for the right answer to emerge.' Waiting is only *sometimes* a good strategy, and it is important to know when those 'sometimes' are.

HOW TO MANAGE YOUR HIGH GREEN

If you over-use this Colour to the severe exclusion of other Colours, then take yourself in hand and extend your range. It is wasteful of your talent to curtail your effectiveness in Green by failing to integrate it with the other Colours. So long as you live predominantly by Green you will seldom make anything happen, because it is the combination of Green with Blue and Red that innovates new ideas. In Britain we have a reputation for producing many inventions (Green) but never actually innovating them (Blue and Red). The fault may well lie not so much with the Blue and Red people (who are usually blamed) as with the Green, who have not learned how to talk with Blue and Red, nor how to express their ideas in ways that others can actually get hold of. High Greens in a curious way are lazy. They are so quick with their own minds that they resent the time it takes to turn thought into action . . . so they don't. Why not find out more about Blue and Red and encourage yourself to develop your thinking in them to empower your Green?

LOW GREEN SCORE

The lack of Green brings the absence of abundance, a non-recognition of opportunity and options. People who under-use their Green get stuck; in habits, convention, custom, tradition, institutionalization, routine, procedure, orderliness. Green squeezed out by Blue and Red means no new directions, no fresh starts, no startling changes, no new horizons. Where there is a lack of Green there is a lack of energy for possibilities. People who are Low Green often have a strong need for certainty. They actively dislike situations where they find themselves having to 'make things up as they go along' or be spontaneous. Instead, they will require 'time to think' – a lot of time, unless they have a decisive Soft Blue component in their emotional make-up. Usually one new idea at a time is their limit for coping with newness. Juggling lots of ideas at once, or darting around from flower to flower like the proverbial bee, is not their forte.

So if you under-use your Green, you may rightly be labelled 'stick-in-the-mud'. Adventure will require you to muster great energy and determination. Your approach is to embark upon anything that is a bit risky with much preparation, forethought, caution and care. An initiative will weigh heavily on you. The chances of casting yourself into the future with anything approaching gay abandon are virtually nil. You call this prudence; others see it as rank conservatism. To be light-hearted and fun-loving requires you to make a supreme effort to switch out of your preference to be responsible about things.

The advantage of having little Green around, though, is that people can get on with the task in hand. They can get down to things. Put Green in abeyance and it actually becomes possible to carry an idea through to see if it will work. Low Greens can be the 'salt-of-the-earth solid citizens'. They are the ones who buckle down to things, accepting situations as they find them rather than trying to change them or escape from them. These people can make the world go round, ensure that seed-time and harvest take place without fail, that mouths are fed and bodies sheltered.

Under-used Hard in Low Green: 'Every problem really is a problem'

People with this sort of low showing in Hard Green may have a rigidity in their thinking which impairs creativity. This could be linked with a tendency to experience every difficulty as a stumbling block because they lack that facility of spirit to get round hold-ups. They plough on in straight lines, so if there is a brick wall in the way they let it stop them. They will 'tut-tut' disapprovingly if a strongly Biased Hard Green colleague suggests they look for ways to break out of or get round the blockage. Their preferred approach is to slog through it and to demolish it, albeit expensively, just because it is 'in the way'.

Those who are low in Hard Green will have their negotiating skills impaired. Hard Green is the necessary ingredient to discover ingenious ways out of confrontation. A little bit of magic from a Hard Green twist to an argument can do wonders to loosen entrenched positions. And the humour of Hard Green can save many a difficult situation – for example, at one extreme during long hours in smoky rooms thrashing out negotiating positions or, in quite a different context, to soften the opposition of a hostile customer.

Under-used Soft in Low Green: 'To do or to be'

If your scorings show up like this then you may well be thanking your lucky stars, since Soft Green people often have a hard time of it in our society. But you are missing out on the rich pastures of imagination. If mental pictures do not come readily to your mind, cultivating your ability to make images will bring rewards. Much that is excitingly creative starts without words.

If really fresh ideas are to bubble up, the mind needs to relax into symbols, into colour, into free-flowing non-verbal movement. Those who encourage their Soft Green to 'come through' allow themselves to 'be'. They let their minds wander deliberately so that things can be revealed to them. They have learnt to be purposefully unpurposeful. They allow beauty, nature, music, growing things to awaken thoughts that cannot come from hard slog and linear logic. Instead, they invite images into the soul by looking at the world without trying to contain or explain. If you think this seems time-wasting, that is your lack of Soft Green speaking. This is the first hurdle to overcome.

HOW TO IMPROVE ON YOUR LOW GREEN

Practise having fun. Practise being irresponsible. Practise saying crazy things from time to time and see the effect. Make yourself take up a wild idea for the sheer fun of it, to break the old patterns of seriousness. You might get to enjoy it, and more to the point, you may find you begin to spark ideas that are worth following through, which in any case you will do admirably with all your Red and Blue. You might also warm to people who are very Green and who normally get your goat, as your understanding and empathy for Green increases.

If you are to practise using Green you must create circumstances when you feel safe to 'play the fool', to let your hair down and say silly things, without caring whether they are right or wrong, good or bad, wise or foolish. The point is, when you are in Green you just don't know whether your idea is sensible, useful or downright nonsense. That's the risk. Green is risky. That's why Green people actually are brave, because they are willing to risk their reputation for the joy and felicity of finding, amongst the myriad ideas they generate, the one or two gold nuggets that will change the world, or at least their small corner of it.

Section Two

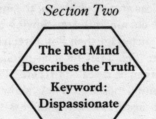

**The Red Mind
Describes the Truth**
**Keyword:
Dispassionate**

Red is the go-between for Green and Blue. Because it strives for truth it can support both the other Colours. It supports Green by giving information to develop ideas and bring them down to earth. It supports Blue by giving it true data and observations which will counterbalance the force of judgement which can wander from reality. This role for the Red mediator is very important in divisive situations.

MID RED SCORE

Truth has many faces. So good Mid Red thinkers employ a wide repertoire of approaches in order to accomplish anything like completeness of knowledge and understand truth in the round. Certain animal-like skills to ferret out what is true are applicable – the eagle's eye, the dog's nose, the elephant's memory, the ant's thoroughness, the mouse's inquisitiveness, the donkey's patience. A good Red thinker uses a wide range, while a poor one relies on just one or two. The latter's perception of truth is therefore rather restricted and lop-sided.

The important characteristic of Mid Red people, as long as they are not biased by a strong Soft Blue component, is their ability to be **Dispassionate**. They have a wonderful capacity to hold in abeyance their personal values and beliefs so that they can investigate and examine issues and problems without their own personal feelings interfering with the fact-finding stage of the inquiry. This quality is a real asset in all dispute cases, especially in a situation where feelings are running high and where the outcome has been pre-judged by most people involved. Mid Red people just want to find out or to tell the truth. They have no desire to pander to the popular opinion, or go with the crowd. Truth is their protection from prejudice, from currying favour and from fear of consequences. Reds want to 'tell it as it is'.

Another valuable attribute of Mid Red characters is their tenacity in holding true to the matter in hand. They are able to identify the level and scope of what they should tackle and stick to it. And as long as they keep any wayward Green elements in their mental make-up under control, they are not readily beguiled into chasing exciting ideas which, although attractive, fall outside the scope of their enquiry.

> ### Hard Bias in Mid Red: 'A place for everything and everything in its place'

People with Hard Red in their mental make-up are neat, down-to-earth, and always willing to tidy up and sort out mess. They like order and must have invented the keynote phrase above. They are a boon whenever there is a fact-finding job to be done. Hard Red essentially **Specifies** and **Categorizes** with precision, accuracy, detail and completeness. The completeness in information which Hard Red looks for is a function of **Look-in**, the ability to examine information that is within the problem, and **Look-out**, to examine also what is surrounding it. In this respect Hard Red takes the *Gestalt* view. It wisely recognizes that when you are engaged in gathering information about a problem you must not only absorb what is immediately relevant (foreground) but also include the background. And vice-versa.

Hard Red thinkers dress neatly. They set up systems at home whereby they ensure that their shoes are polished in rota, their shirts and suits are worn in rota, and when the weather changes they will be prepared. It is as if they all had a good scouting training in their youth. The army instils Hard Red virtues which once learned become difficult to throw off because they are routinized. Good routine is the hall-mark of well-managed Hard Red thinking. It can be learned.

Soft Bias in Mid Red: 'Things are not always as they appear'

This phrase is chosen because it conveys the complexity of this Mode of thinking. Soft Red seeks to reveal what lies within appearances, so that truth really appears. It seeks to discover not what is obvious but what is implicit, hidden. You often hear people say, 'There's something odd about the atmosphere in that place.' They are expressing something they have picked up through their Soft Red antennae – if you asked them precisely what is odd they would be hard put to explain. But they have received an impression of 'something', below the surface of the walls, the tables, chairs, carpets, which told them the place was 'odd'. Things are not always what they seem.

You enter Soft Red when seeking to penetrate below the surface of things, that is, appearances, in order to discover what really is there. But only when you genuinely seek to do it, without distorting the truth through your own (Soft Blue) interpretations. Remember, Red is **Dispassionate**. The intention of Soft Red is to find out what is truly going on, what is actually happening, what really exists that is not immediately apparent. It is a fine line between observation and interpretation. Soft Red has the intention to **Observe**, so must be wary of personal interpretations which do not reflect the evidence, however slight, that is available.

People who favour the use of their Soft Red cultivate all their faculties – eyes, ears, taste, smell, touch, kinesthetic sense, sense of heat and cold, sense of pain and well-being, so that they become effective 'readers' of implicit truth. Their different senses, alerted to perceive what is going on either inside themselves or in the situation around them, inform them of layers below layers of reality. In order to ascertain which layers (or levels) to take into account and which to discount, they make use of their ability to gauge the level of complexity they handle at any one time.

The sensitivity of Soft Reds to impressions given off by people, places, buildings and things also sharpens their sensitivity to the impressions they give to others. They are aware of how they come across, and take care about the things they say and write, the clothes they wear, the way they speak and so on. They are interested in how they **Code** to others and how others 'Code' to them. People in Advertising, Journalism, Fashion and Design are high on this.

HIGH RED SCORE

While truth can never be found or fixed for all time, the quest for truth springs eternal in the soul. This is the intention which energizes Red thinking. High Reds carry this to extremes. We know someone who enjoys studying volumes of railway and airline timetables. However long the road, however costly in terms of personal effort, individuals who rate Red highly will work on and on until they discover the answers that satisfy their inner demand to find out. The drawback here is that High Reds may never be satisfied. For them, truth is a never-ending quest. They will avoid ever coming to a conclusion, pleading that they need to get more information before they can make up their mind . . . very frustrating for colleagues or marriage partners. And they will bore you with endless lists and details, because for High Hard Red it is essential that you know absolutely everything. (Unless of course you are also High Hard Red, in which case you will both be in your element.)

If the hallmark of a Mid Red is a dispassionate nature, the High Red person is passionate about being dispassionate. This is a wonderful asset when the task requires it, but when it takes on the cold unemotional tone of detachment, it is upsetting to be on the receiving end. Those with a High Red component need to ask themselves whether they are sometimes guilty of giving the unvarnished truth when tact might be more appropriate.

Hard Bias in High Red: 'The truth, the whole truth and nothing but the truth'

The trouble with Hard Red is that it suffers from a hardening of the categories. Once it has established its own definitions of truth, its own constructs within which it will view the world, it will only see the world that way. When it looks for the truth it looks for nothing but the truth as defined by its own categories. The saddest instance of this in our society is found in the medical profession's categorization of what is 'scientific', and therefore 'proper and safe' in medicine, and what is not. Doctors dish out to their patients tranquillizers and sedatives which, though they have been scientifically tested and passed as 'safe', have caused harmful addictions in many thousands of people. Meanwhile, traditional herbal remedies which do not induce harmful addictions have been denigrated as unscientific and dismissed from western medical practice because they were not invented in a test-tube by a pharmaceutical company. In this instance, the medical profession has formed a category of thinking which allies 'scientific' with 'tested' and 'safe' and ignores treatments developed and used for centuries whose benefits, though experienced by many people, often cannot be explained.

Another side of over-done Hard Red is its pedantic dullness when it becomes over-routinized. The neat accounting for everything, the scrupulous adherence to schedules, the desire for everyone and everything to be 'in place', results in working systems that choke creativity with proceduralization – for instance, the bureaucratic structures of the civil service, the authoritarian structures of the military, or the mechanized structures of the factory. The human spirit becomes dulled in such atmospheres and seeks escape in rebellion. It is a curious tight-rope. Without the Hard Red qualities of faithfulness to accuracy and truth, our commercial and industrial systems would have no basis for trading, for there would be no means of accounting. Yet this same positive quality when misapplied does untold damage to our social life at work.

Such a Bias in Hard Red must watch out for tendencies to be nit-picky, over-long on data and short on sensitivity to other people's time-span of attention, and finally, rigid towards change.

Soft Bias in High Red: 'The medium is the message'

You can go too far along the Code route, reaching the absurdity of the phrase above. The strength of Soft Red is that it takes care to 'package', but over-packaging leads everyone up the garden path. It may be fair-dos that the packaging for perfume costs more than the contents of the bottle, but when three screws are 'packaged' in polythene and cardboard cut-outs so that the packaging costs more than the screws, we have gone beyond good sense for supposed convenience at point of sale. We have neglected Blue judgement in favour of Soft Red impressions.

Of course, it is all a matter of priorities, but Soft Red can go overboard on appearances, thus disguising instead of il-luminating the appearance of truth. The classic children's story *Little Women* tells of the heroine's first taste of high society. At her first appearance she wore a simple dress. 'Kind' friends suggested she would reveal herself to greater advantage if she allowed them to lend her a dress for the next dance. They made her up, refashioned her hair, bedecked her with jewellery to offset the borrowed finery. Flushed in her new-found elegance, she was dismayed to overhear two gentlemen refer-ring to her new 'look' with disappointment. For them her natural beauty was spoiled.

Overdone Soft Red's other serious fault is its tendency *never* to be specific. It is as if Hard Red is such a bore that people who are high in Soft Red just can't be bothered to get down to the nitty-gritty. Soft Red people can be disastrously woolly. For example, they can arrive for a briefing on a project and listen with absorption and interest but never take a note. They are relying on their memory (as Red people do). But because they do not have that precision of Hard Red to support their thinking they are fuzzy on remembering the details of what was required or agreed. Unless they are well trained, designers, architects, interior decorators (usually high on Soft Red) can be extremely difficult to brief. There is a genuine fear on their part that if they tie their minds down to details they will lose their sense of the whole. So the sensible client writes it all down for them to ensure that there is a record of exactly what is to be achieved.

HOW TO MANAGE YOUR HIGH RED

What a High Red thinker must bear in mind is balancing the Red's consuming need to get to the bottom of everything with the practicalities of time-constraints, resources available and the sensitivities of other people involved. So if you are high in Red, activate your Blue to select to what depth you should be working at any one time.

In fact, it is Blue that comes to the rescue of Red when it is going over the top by burying everyone in information. Whether it be facts or impressions, figures or anecdotes, the Red person has to learn to judge (Blue) what is relevant for whom. Blue is the Red mind's arbiter of appropriateness and should be cultivated to help manage an overpreponderance of Red.

LOW RED SCORE

When Red is lacking, an awful lot of nonsense can be talked. There is a lack of realism, a lack of interest in how things really are. People who are low in Red won't bother to find out even most easily obtained information because they are not attracted to putting effort into it. Their own ignorance does not upset them. They feel, frankly, that it's a bore, a mundane job which they can delegate to a subordinate. People who lack Red often have a high propensity for giving their opinions and ideas gratuitously, regardless of whether there is any substance of truth in them.

People who are low in Red will show the other Colours in their more unfavourable lights. Their Blue views come through as opinionated because they lack a grounding in truth. Their Green ideas never get any flesh put on them because the low Red component fails to bring forward the necessary data. They may well be seen by others as reckless in their disregard for information.

What advantages are there in having a low Red component in your make-up? You will never be prone to that terrible disease of information constipation. You certainly won't be the one to hold up decisions with demands to accumulate more and more about less and less. Nor will you hide behind the cry: 'I can't possibly decide on this as I don't have enough information.'

Under-used Hard in Low Red: 'Oh sorry, I forgot . . . lost it . . . can't find it . . .'

The signs of a lack of Hard Red are a messy desk, lost files, scrappy records, spelling mistakes, sloppy dressing, unpolished shoes, and forgetfulness. These are meant to be the faults of adolescence but for some of us things do not change when we become adults. You can always recognize the home of a person who is low in Hard Red: last year's newspapers in the magazine rack; last year's frozen peas buried under this year's in the freezer; every surface littered with clutter.

More annoying, at work they will never remember what you might expect any normal person to. They forget where they put things, forget who said what, when, forget when they last did something, forget even what they were last doing. If this person is to function at all effectively in a work environment it is essential that he is trained to use lists and diaries to keep track of his progress and commitments.

Under-used Soft in Low Red: 'Call a spade a spade'

Those who are low in Soft Red will lack an appreciation of the subtleties of impressions given and received below the level of what is obvious. First they fail to notice and pick up what is significant but not overtly plain. Secondly, they will not have the qualities we normally associate with good diplomacy, namely the ability to be able to adjust their dress and language to suit the occasion. They are likely to believe it is important to 'be themselves' and to call a spade a spade whatever situation they find themselves in.

Without Soft Red in their make-up people lack sensitivity to what is appropriate. Not only in terms of relating to people, but also in terms of 'sensing' the appropriate level to be working on. These are what we might term political (with a small 'p') sensitivities. This also applies when tackling any kind of problem. They may well use a sledge-hammer to crack a nut or fail to bring in the big guns or tackle the issue at a sufficiently high conceptual level when required.

HOW TO IMPROVE ON YOUR LOW RED

Since Red is the Colour that principally links Green and Blue it is important for Low Reds to learn to value it. Which means allowing themselves to give the time to those who need to know more. Impatience must be curbed. Time spent in Red is not time wasted. It is not wasting other people's time either to ask them for and tell them information.

Of all the Colours, Red probably requires the most time. Indeed, people probably devote more time to managing and resourcing Red than any other Colour. Red is the Colour of communication at all levels. It is the basis of bureaucracy, systems, procedures, accounts, money dealing – all of which provide the structures within which trade and commerce take place. Literature, journalism and documentary depend on Red. It is the basis of gossip, of rumour, of being 'in the know' and of getting the message across. It is all Red information. Red thinking is the raw material of the world of work.

Start to notice how working-life is based in Red, in communicating information of all kinds. Don't we speak of this as the age of Information Technology? Those who want to rise in their careers need to ensure a very steady and sure grasp of Red. It is all about being informed. A democracy that is uninformed cannot be a real democracy. Knowledge is potential power. When Red thinking is given direction from Blue thinking, then there is power through purpose.

Section Three

The Blue Mind
Judges What is Right
Keyword:
Discriminate

The theme of Blue is forming judgement, in readiness to take action. Green thinking generates the different possibilities open to you, Red supplies you with the necessary information, and Blue discriminates between the better and the worse alternatives.

MID BLUE SCORE

Everyone makes lots of decisions all day and every day. They are using their Blue capacities to do this. A balanced Blue mind brings qualities of probing questions, honest opinion and sober foresight. These are the bed-rock for sound moral decisions which we hope lie at the core of social, business and political activity.

People who like to use their Blue thinking and have mastered some of its skills are usually found in leadership roles. They lead through their ability to weigh risk, assess expectations and hone down argument to its core considerations, and by their willingness to come down on one side or the other, to make decisions and take action.

A balanced Blue thinking capacity is usually recognized as good management material, for at the heart of management is judgement: judgement about people, about timing, about good practice, quality, money, material resources. Luck plays its part, but people who are in tune with their faculties of judgement win their own luck for themselves. When choosing marshals to command his army, Napoleon is said to have demanded: 'Give me officers who have been lucky in the field.'

> **Hard Bias in Mid Blue: 'Let us first of all follow reason, it is the surest guide. It warns us itself of its feebleness and informs us of its own limitations' – Anatole France**

Reason is normally held to be the most significant thinking power in the western world. Why it is powerful is summed up in the above quotation. It holds within itself its own justification. It cannot be contradicted from another thinking Colour because it does not recognize the validity of any thought process other than rational logic. So it has to learn to live alongside other thinking approaches, and this a balanced Hard Blue can do.

The rational mind has to follow certain procedures if the laws of logic are to be obeyed. It must at all times maintain an objective stance, never allowing personal feelings or values to cloud the purity of the logic of its data. All its energies are directed towards resolving the correct answer to a question by purely analytical steps. First, it must **Compare** whatever statements or evidence is available. Then it must **Distinguish** from the evidence what is significant or pertinent to the question. Finally, it must **Test** its conclusions with rigorous logic, play devil's advocate, in order to ensure that there has been no flaw in any of the deductions.

Hard Blue, when it is well managed, is penetrating, able to sift the wheat from the chaff and to cut through clever claptrap with razor sharpness. It is the invaluable tool in all management jobs where information has to be checked for validity before it is applied. It is ineffective to trust that the negotiator across the table has put together an entirely logical case. His argument must be put to the test using all the powers of Hard Blue.

Soft Bias in Mid Blue: '*Le coeur a ses raisons, que la raison ne connaît point*' – Pascal (The heart has its reasons of which Reason has no knowledge at all.)

While Hard Blue seeks to operate from an objective standpoint, Soft Blue is the opposite. Soft Blue minds wish to align all that they do with what they **Value** as individuals. Personal criteria are paramount. Soft Blue people decide how they will act through their own feelings of what is good and bad, what is just and unjust, what is right and wrong. This is what is important for them. Objective argument may be taken into account, but when the chips are down their subjective values, not logic, will impel them to **Commit** to a decision.

What does this mean? Soft Blue is often typified as a female attribute, where thinking is ruled by the heart, and is opposed to Hard Blue which is seen as male and arising from the head. (The discerning reader will see that this is in no way a sexist remark.) There is a genuine opposition between Hard and Soft

Blue, but there is also a wonderful synergy which the balanced Soft Blue can make the most of. Every Hard Blue logical argument must finally be weighed against human values, which cannot be culled from logic alone. Logic does not understand ideals, it does not understand kindness, or forgiveness, or love. Logic appreciates neither the joy of comradeship nor generosity in adversity. While you may argue a case logically, what really impels action is personal commitment. Energy comes from Soft not Hard Blue. If we lose sight of this, our work is dehumanized and we become alienated.

We sometimes hear people complaining that their colleagues, or their shop-floor workers, or their directors 'simply do not listen to reason'. By this they think they mean Reason . . . logic. But all too often they actually mean reasons, values, their own point of view or common sense. Those they are talking to are listening for what they value, what they want, and they hear their own values ignored or violated. We all have to watch the tendency to think that our Soft Blue reasons are Hard Blue Reason. It is a slip of mind which has serious consequences throughout all levels of society.

People can respond when they can connect a message to their own aspirations, their own desires, their own longings – all Soft Blue stuff. Pure Reason must therefore be **Interpreted,** worked over, and adapted to meet different situations. What is more, managers have to find ways to incorporate unreasoned reasons into the logic systems of their organizations. We have the phrase 'bend the rules', and bureaucrats need to do this more often because we know that the logic of bureaucratic systems cannot encompass the variety of human values.

If logic ruled the day, we would never take a risk. A risk, by definition, means that you cannot **Predict** the outcome. Yet Soft Blue has this marvellous willingness to try to predict, to have a best guess, to lay its bets, and on that basis to restrain itself or launch forth into action.

HIGH BLUE SCORE

Be careful if you are High in Blue. These people can leap in too often too quickly with a ready-made decision, without having really looked for options (Green) or gathered sufficient information (Red) to back up the decision. It is typical of strong Blue people that they 'make their minds up' about something very quickly and immediately put it into operation. This can come across as decisive management, firm leadership, and purposeful problem-solving, which can work very well in unchanging, repetitive situations. But that kind of leadership is disastrous where circumstances are changing. Ready-made judgements are then inappropriate. Far too much British management operates in the pragmatic mould, where experience is judge. Experience is only a good judge when the situation is comparable with previous ones.

A danger with High Blue is that its capacity to discriminate (neutral) becomes discrimination (prejudice). High Blues can adopt a prejudiced stance on an issue because they do not trouble to take into account fresh information and ideas. Most of us suffer from fixed views in one department of our life or another, but High Blue people are more opinionated than most and less willing to present an open mind at the outset. They take a lot of 'persuading'. However, once convinced they are stalwarts for sticking with it and seeing it through.

High Blues will be impatient to get on with things so they get irritated with Green people who like to speculate on possibilities and explore more openings. They also get impatient with Red people who take time in meetings to tell you the background and want to take longer to collate further data. Narrow-minded Soft Blues have a strange reverse effect on their desire for action. They sometimes say no to a new idea immediately, to rule it out of court, which stops any action at all. This is maddening to the Green person who is impatient to get his idea adopted. Of course, Red and Green are High Blue's allies, if Blue handles them well. Usually though, Blue sees them as terrible time-wasters. High Blue, you see, feels impelled by an overriding inner obligation to make the decision now, and to take action immediately. Naturally, this cuts down the invaluable contributions from Red and Green thinking.

> **Hard Bias in High Blue: 'I can stand brute force, but brute reason is quite unbearable. There is something unfair about its use. It is hitting below the intellect.' – Oscar Wilde**

When Hard Blue goes over the top it can wound and destroy. Logic is not always appropriate but some folk use it for overkill. The ruthless pursuit of logic can crush, for example, the less robust thinking powers of Green and Soft Red. Emerging Green ideas, new-born and fragile, will be smashed to smithereens under the advancing artillery of Hard Blue, while Soft Red's reliance on the intangible, on the implicit, will get short shrift. Hard Red stands up to Hard Blue through the strength of its dependence on measurable fact, so these two are often found in cahoots.

This Bias in Hard Blue can come across as aggression – although the intention may be simply to test the soundness of what is being said. If the recipient of testing questions does not understand the nature of testing, which aims to examine not the person but the information, then sparks fly and feelings can be hurt.

These Hard Blue types can walk around with two flat feet, stepping onto painful soft spots, with a complete lack of sensitivity. And why? Because they have all their attention focused to strike to the core of an issue's integrity, to dissect the parts, to discard irrelevancies and to produce a well-honed argument for or against. Concern for people's feelings, concern for the intangible niceties of life, appreciation of the relevance of 'irrelevancies' does not figure in their way of approaching problems. Not for nothing was it called 'Occam's razor' – the dictum of the 14th-century philosopher, which says that you should believe only that which requires fewest assumptions.

So, High Hard Blues are wonderful interrogators, maintaining firm objectivity, but giving the appearance of lack of compassion. The Devil's Advocate has an archetypal Hard Blue Biased approach. His aim is to prove beyond any measure of doubt that a saintly person is worthy to be canonized. The other very positive side of the coin becomes apparent here. The more severe the test the more confidence when the 'saint' passes it.

A delightful verse from Oliver Hereford in his *Metaphysics* puts it like this:

> *Why and Wherefore set out one day*
> *To hunt for a wild Negation,*
> *They agreed to meet at a cool retreat*
> *On the Point of Interrogation.*

Soft Bias in High Blue: 'He makes black white and white he turns to black' – Ovid

---

Beware! These may be dangerous waters when you tread them in this Bias. Soft Blue may want something so much that it does not stop at bending the rules but breaks them. Strong Soft Blues lead rebellions because their belief system, value, dominates all logic (Hard Blue) and overturns truth (Red). Against all odds they will predict success and no matter what assails them they will interpret all signs to be in their favour. They will commit even their lives. Kamikaze pilots, self-igniting Buddhists, IRA terrorists, gurus, evangelists – all those with a cause bigger than themselves with which they have completely identified.

Closer to home we see this behaviour with less stark examples, but in their own way equally powerful: the mother who dedicates her life to her handicapped child to the neglect of the rest of her children and her husband; the entrepreneur who so drives himself for his business that he drops dead at 35; the teenage athlete who is so set on becoming the champion that he despises all schooling that does not feed his success; the unemployed person who is so locked into despair that he refuses to accept what help is offered because it is not an immediate and complete solution.

In all these cases we see the powerful Soft Blue Bias subjecting individuals to the tyranny of their own beliefs. When Soft Blue takes over, it can create demons or saints, but both border on madness and both need to bring their other Colours into play in order to balance the extremes.

A far more common experience of this Bias in Soft Blue is found in the over-hasty rush to get on with things. Impatience might be a synonym for it. The mind immediately wants to resolve a dilemma with action rather than with thinking. So no chance is given for fresh alternatives, and important information may be ignored. Another danger with Soft Blue is that it distorts, interprets what it reads, sees and hears to fit what it wants to believe. Probably all of us are guilty of this when it suits us, but a biased person would not notice what he has done and would not feel any sense of guilt because he would take his interpretation to be right.

HOW TO MANAGE YOUR HIGH BLUE

Establish your priorities and manage your time better, so that your compulsive urge to 'close' on an issue can be withheld by your own good self-management. All too often, urgency and importance are mixed in together thus confusing instead of clarifying what actions need to be taken when. When prioritizing, use information about urgency (Red) to modify or support your judgement of importance (Blue). In this way you can relax your impatience when it is not needed. This will make room for the Red and Green to have their say.

The biggest step a High Blue has to take is to learn to respect and value the other thinking Colours. Judgemental Blue is tempted to too much pride in its own powers. It needs a gentler touch and to learn from the qualities that the other Colours exemplify, so that its raw energy is not destructive of the harmony of wholeness and the creativity of exploration.

LOW BLUE SCORE

It has to be remembered that the essence of Blue is its drive towards commitment to action, towards singling out the one course of action that it is right to take. Without a goodly portion of Blue in your mental make-up you will probably dither or delay when it comes to making up your mind. Low Blues are likely to want circumstances to sort themselves, without having to make a positive choice one way or another.

They avoid choosing by a variety of strategies, depending upon the strength of the other Colours in their thinking style. For example, someone with Low Blue coupled with High Red will resort to gathering information, in the fond hope that if they collect enough of it the decision will be made by the sheer weight of the evidence. This is not an efficient decision process. By contrast, someone who is Low Blue coupled with High Green will indulge in their favourite pastime of thinking up more and more alternatives, expecting one to jump forth that will sparkle as *the* solution through some mysterious chemistry of attraction.

Commitment, then, is not a Low Blue's strong point. This means that Low Blue people will not take kindly to being pinned down and required to account for their actions. They like to have the scope to explore in Red and Green without being contained in the whys and wherefores of purpose. And if you lack Blue, watch out that you are not driving your Blue comrades to distraction by your unwillingness to keep to a time-scale. Getting things done on time will not come naturally to you, unless you have been well schooled by your education and training to meet deadlines.

There is a looseness in a Low Blue's thinking which allows scope for Red and Green to function without the constraints of the Blue mind's desire for aims and goals. When there is need for this kind of freedom it pays dividends. But when it results in lack of direction it dissipates energy.

Under-used Hard in Low Blue: 'Never mind the why and wherefore' – W. S. Gilbert.

People who are low in Hard Blue can be very slow and inefficient about getting things done because they lack the ability to distinguish the essential from the important. They may try to do everything without identifying priorities or they may leave out essential things because they haven't identified them as having the kind of importance that is absolute. They lack that icy sharpness which sorts objectively the essentials from the non-essentials. These people may be led into highways and byways by their own enthusiasms or by other people's, which deviate and possibly detract from whatever purpose they have in hand. This strategy is only acceptable when there is no time limit and no constraint on resources, for example, in a leisure activity or an open-ended research project.

People who under-use their Hard Blue may be very susceptible to plausible argument, since they are low on that ability to ask penetrating questions which so marks out Hard Blue. They allow their minds to be attracted and caught in one aspect which appeals to or interests them so that it overwhelms all consideration of checking its rationale, or placing it within the context of the whole story.

We may well thank Heaven for these people in our world today, for they act not out of calculation of costs and benefits but can respond from their human interest. In our institutionalized, bureaucratized, and systematized life-styles we probably need a goodly dose of inefficient Low Hard Blue. This creates room for those chance happenings when, by marvellous serendipity, something wonderful comes together which logic and reason could never have brought about. A diet of nothing but high-protein Hard Blue with no roughage gets you awfully constipated.

> **Under-used Soft in Low Blue: 'Will you, won't you, will you, won't you, will you join the dance?' – Lewis Carroll**

Vacillation denotes a lack of Soft Blue. Those who lack it find their urge to commit is not pronounced and the strength of what they value does not impel them forward to action. This delay over decision-taking does not reflect the wisdom of waiting for the opportune moment, for that requires a positive choice not to act yet. There is a difference between not making a choice and choosing not to do something. Without Soft Blue, people just dither.

They are probably not joiners, because believing 'in' something in order to belong to a group is not their cup of tea. However, they can cope with a group that allows them to pursue an interest without requiring them to 'belong'. Any group that is concerned with collecting things is likely to appeal, for example, collecting Victoriana, old books, or musical boxes, or the kind of bird-spotting that does not demand any passionate expressions of loyalty or devotion.

Those low in Soft Blue like to play it cool. You may think that they don't care – and at a personal level they may not be bothered by much. They have a lot of resistance to being persuaded. They are a salesman's nightmare. They will keep themselves to themselves when it comes to emotions and do not let on to any weakness of want or need.

HOW TO IMPROVE ON YOUR LOW BLUE

Low Blue people need to watch their weakness of purpose and structure. Like High Blue people, they will also benefit from time-management training, but for different reasons. Low Blue types really *must* adopt a good diary system to manage their minds and the tasks they have to do. It should be comprehensive – including work, home and leisure so that a good balance can be struck. Low Blue people can fall prey to such poor management of their time that they fail to apportion realistic time scales to tasks. Nothing gets completed. Someone else, usually a Blue marriage partner or a Blue colleague, has to pick up the pieces all the time.

Small exercises in commitment will strengthen your Blue. A difficult but powerful exercise is this one: pick a time of day, say 3.00 pm, and commit yourself to remembering to stop whatever you are doing at 3.00 on the dot to perform some simple act – like taking a ring off your finger and putting it on again. (Something like that can be done in almost any circumstances so it should not interfere with your work.) Don't use a digital alarm to remind you. Use the power of your own mind. Some people find that it takes them weeks before they can remember to stop. When you have actually remembered for five days in a row, switch to another time and see what happens. Keep a note of the days when you remember and record why you failed.

Another exercise is to make a commitment to do something for someone else every day – and do it, whatever gets in your way. When you fail, examine why. An exercise with a different purpose might be to adopt some little system or method that ensures you will not do something unwise. How do you check your actions for soundness before you take them? Such little acts of self-discipline build your inner resources and self-knowledge and actually strengthen your Blue. Your strengthened Blue then operates in other areas of your life. It is a bit like jogging every morning for 10 minutes. Your muscles are strengthened, your circulation and stamina improve and you have more energy for your work.

CHAPTER FIVE

Guessing Thinking Styles

What's the use of knowing the Colours? Obviously they can help you to understand yourself and others better. What practical use is that? There are two major advantages. The first is to do with managing relationships with people: working for example with customers, subordinates, colleagues, superiors, or living with your family. The second is to do with what particular thinking styles are useful for. If, for example, you are predominantly a Blue thinker, how does this benefit you?

In this chapter we start to look at these advantages and then suggest ways in which you can roughly work out what other people's thinking styles are. This is necessary if you are to be able to co-ordinate your knowledge of your style with other people's. Subsequent chapters take these themes much further and deeper.

USING THINKING STYLES FOR MANAGING RELATIONSHIPS

Consider just how often you are called upon to understand another person in order to achieve something important.

* Selecting someone for a job
* Resolving a difficult relationship (perhaps with your boss)
* Selling your company's products
* Selling your house
* Negotiating a contract for your company or for yourself
* Buying a house
* Getting on with your neighbour (flat-mate, wife) day-in, day-out

* Helping your children cope with school, e.g. understanding their teachers
* Creating a project team from among your colleagues
* Succeeding in a job interview
* Succeeding in getting someone you fancy to say 'yes'
* Passing a promotion board
* Managing meetings
* Picking someone to collaborate with you on a special job

Everyone generates their own ways of 'sussing' other people in order to get along better with them, so that life and work can progress with some degree of efficiency and effectiveness. Business has got wise to this in recent years, making use of the many methods now available for identifying personality profiles to improve recruitment, appraisal and promotion of staff. Indeed, most of us will have some familiarity with such testing, even if only through magazines which nowadays run personality quizzes as regular features. These quizzes can be great fun and extremely useful for giving a quick appreciation of personality.

The idea of a 'thinking profile', to illumine what makes people tick at a deeper level than personality and to show how thinking affects interpersonal relations, is something new. The questionnaires in this book are rather like magazine quizzes: a useful way of giving you a 'feel' of your thinking style so that you can apply what you read here to yourself and to others. We have designed a fully fledged thinking inventory comparable to psychological personality profiles, for organizations and individuals who want to find out about thinking styles in depth, so as to improve management performance. This is the JDR Thinking Intentions Profile (TIP), and all the results are held and analysed on our computer. TIP is for people in organizations, supported by our training programmes and manuals.

To take your investigations into thinking styles further, there is a section later in this chapter on guessing other people's Colours. This gives you ways of roughly working out the key features of people's styles. You can apply this knowledge to situations where collaboration is important. You will find Chapters Six and Seven useful if you want to examine in some depth the interplay between different thinking styles.

WHAT IS YOUR THINKING STYLE GOOD FOR?

The most obvious application is for choosing a job that suits your style, and selecting people so that they naturally fit a job. The approach taken here gives you a quick way of assessing some fundamental characteristics of jobs in terms of Colours. Imagine the casting director for a popular soap-opera choosing actors to fit stereotypes of different jobs portrayed in the series. Here is the stereotyping of the Colours for those jobs.

Hard Blue and Hard Red:
  Engineer, systems analyst, bank clerk, laboratory assistant, surveyor, accountant

Soft Blue and Soft Red:
  Salesman, teacher, nurse, social worker

Soft Red and Hard Red:
  Actor, musician, doctor, gardener, architect, solicitor, secretary, shop keeper, sales assistant, reporter, biographer, policeman

Soft Red and Hard Green:
  Advertising copywriter, barrister, magazine columnist, novelist

Soft Green and Soft Red:
  Marketing manager, company director, poet

Hard Blue and Soft Red:
  Administrator, judge

Why not have a go at casting for the following combinations of Colours?

> Hard Blue and Hard Green
> Soft Blue and Soft Green
> Hard Red and Hard Green
> Hard Blue and Soft Green

Of course, these do not exhaust the possible combinations.

Typecasting presents some obvious dilemmas. What kind of doctors are we thinking of as Soft Red and Hard Red? There is the general practitioner who requires Soft Red for his communication with patients and Hard Red for prescriptions for complaints. A registrar might be much more oriented to Hard Red and Hard Blue for deeper diagnostic skills. Placing a top Civil Service Administrator in the Hard Blue, Soft Red category may be appropriate, but not for the desk-bound office administrator in an engineering firm. He's much more likely to be Hard Red, Hard Blue. And the accountant who is promoted to become finance director had better temper his Hard Red, Hard Blue if he is to meet the demands of the much broader sweep of his new job. He will need Hard Green and Soft Red.

Our stereotypes are a useful beginning to examining jobs. To do it properly one must look in some depth at the particular job or class of jobs. There are engineering consultants, for example, who really do need to have Hard Red, Hard Blue as their leading thinking skills. Others, who tackle tasks with a much broader range, require their Hard Green and even Soft Red to be at the fore. They must have a sufficient level of Hard Blue, Hard Red skill to meet basic technical competence but they also need the added magic of Hard Green, for example, to cope with leading-edge technology.

This raises two interesting issues: promotion and selection for jobs. The Peter Principle (which says that people are promoted to jobs that are just above the one they can competently do) can be thwarted with a proper grasp of thinking styles. Competence is often to do with the matching of someone's leading Colours to the thinking requirements of a

particular job. Promote them and their new job no longer
matches. If they do not have sufficient elasticity in their
Colours to adapt and extend their range (see Chapter Eight)
they will not be effective, especially if the job pivots around
certain key Colours. For example, there are far too many
company directors who operate with leading Colours that were
an excellent match below Board level but inappropriate for the
real tasks of directing a company.

Selection for jobs as we all know is crucial for the satisfaction
of the person in the job and for the effective execution of it.
Some jobs remain the same over decades and through force of
habit companies get good at recruiting satisfactorily into them.
What if times change? Then you need to look for people with
different Colours to change the character of jobs. The impetus
to change can then come from the different kinds of thinking
energies of the new recruits. They think differently and they
will therefore change what is done and how. If this option isn't
open to you then ways have to be found to extend the scope of
the thinking styles of the people 'in situ'. Extending the
capabilities of thinking is dealt with in Chapter Eight.

Here we have taken a glimpse at the implications of the
Colours for job analysis, recruitment, selection, appraisal and
promotion. Since jobs are not unified wholes but comprise
many facets which require different thinking energies, this is
taken up in more depth later in the book.

HOW YOUR STYLE AFFECTS THE WAY YOU READ THIS BOOK

Everyone's 'peculiar' style is good for something. Take an
immediate example of reading a book – reading this book. Each
person's style will lead them to approach the book in different
ways, giving them special advantages (and of course some
limitations).

The rule-of-thumb sketches below do not predict accurately
how you will read the book because you are not just 'one' Colour
but a combination. However, they illustrate how significant
Colours in your style affect the way you tackle it. Read up on all

the approaches; see what your combination is and note what you are missing.

High in Hard Blue If Hard Blue predominates in your thinking style, you will want to cross-check, question and test the validity of what is presented. You will probably often find yourself in dispute with ideas here. You will be pleased when arguments are logically presented or you can connect one statement with another in straightforward deduction. Analogies and examples may annoy you because they will seem to you to be unnecessary embroidery. Diagrams that are well presented, to enhance the clarity of the argument, will be acceptable to you, but not necessary. You may well skip them. If you find the argument of the book is sound and strong you will form a judgement that approves and uses its content. If you dispute the argument and it cannot satisfactorily answer outstanding questions then you will throw it out. Before taking such a drastic step make sure you read Chapter Ten which gives you the research basis to the book. This will be important to you and will carry far more weight in your mind than many diagrams, exercises and illustrations.

High in Soft Blue With a Soft Blue component that is significant in your thinking style, you will be concerned to identify whether the values put forward in this book actually match your own. And you may have some quick firm objectives you want it to satisfy. Although the Model of the Colours is value-free, this may actually make it unattractive to you because values are so central to your thinking. You will be searching out to discover our values as authors, to read them between the lines. Since values are so individual, some of what we believe in is bound to tally with your own ideals, and some may well differ. The practical illustrations of the Colours of Thinking at work will be a source of interest for you since they will reveal how the Colours affect people's beliefs and behaviour. The examples bring the conceptual model of thinking to life.

High in Hard Red The detail of the book will be important to you. You may even try to read this whole reference chapter straight through. You are most likely to complete the exercises in it, because your thoroughness will cause you to proceed systematically from one chapter to another, completing each section so that you can put it tidily away before moving onto the next. If you discover any inconsistencies in the layout or format, or any proof errors, that will be a black mark against the book. You will also notice any slips in references, and be annoyed by them. The neatness of the diagrams, the exercises and the details of content will also impact you and if we have not met your high standards your opinion of the book may be adversely affected.

High in Soft Red You will take the broad sweep approach; you will flip through chapters to light on the ones that immediately appeal to your way of looking at life. Your eye will be attracted to illustrations and images and you will read round them, grasping the message of the book by dipping into it, doing the odd exercise here and there, reflecting on the meaning of a paragraph or two and colouring in the odd page to bring the images of the Colours alive. You will enjoy the introductory chapter which gives you an overview of the book and Chapter Ten on the research background. You will feel quite happy if you end up with the essential message of the book.

High in Hard Green With your interest in making new connections, you will devour the book for its ideas which you can pinch to make use of in your own life. You will take the descriptive list of contents as a useful source from which you can pull out all the ideas on a particular theme so that you can play with them, build on them and put them together to form something satisfactory for your own uses. Your drive will be to turn what is presented here into something that is your own creation, a bit different. You should find this book a fund of ideas ripe for plagiarizing with a light heart.

High in Soft Green You will be hoping for a vision of something new, something that brings fresh insight, that illumines your mind and life and takes it to a new plane. The Model itself brings that. Here you will find ways of gaining permission for the wonderful quality of Soft Green thinking. With the simplicity of the Model of the Colours, which combines within it the complexity of all human thought, you can stretch your imagination to see the possibilities that lie ahead when society accepts and makes use of the power of Soft Green thinking. You may even draw inspiration for bringing it through.

MAKE THE COLOURS AN AID FOR READING AND STUDY

Whatever your preferred thinking style, colour brings black and white linear text alive. Now you have a colour coding which combines in itself added depth of meaning. The Colours are a universal language; they are present in all languages, all texts, pictures, presentations, dramas, poems, conversation and in all behaviour.

1. Colour the diagrams. Repetition ingrains the coding of the Colours into your memory.

2. Colour-mark the book whenever one of the Colours stands out significantly. Do it to reports, newspapers, or advertisements, guessing which Colour is being used when. Of course one or other of the Colours is in use all the time, since all thinking is in Colour, but we are not advocating the obliteration of texts with Colour markings! Just highlight what is significant. 'Colour' highlighting of this kind is an ingenious tool for revealing structure in written material and helps to clarify which kinds of thinking *are* being used and which *are not*. It is a decoding device for identifying the intentions of the writer.

3. Use the same Colour highlighting on your own writing. Colour code is a powerful tool for analysing your own style and identifying what you need to add or subtract in order to improve.

How to Guess Someone's Thinking Style

Since one is used to describing other people by their personality traits – 'She's an extrovert', 'He's rather shy', 'He's a hot-tempered so-and-so' – it takes a little time to get used to looking for thinking traits. You have to do some double guessing to penetrate beneath personality. Most important to remember is that exterior personality may hide or cloak thinking styles, so it is necessary to look and listen below the surface. To draw an analogy from nature, when first looking at a rushing river it seems all chaos and turmoil. But by watching persistently over a period of time you begin to see how the underlying river-bed of rocks and reeds causes the river to flow in particular ways. The first chaotic impression gradually gives way to an appreciation of pattern in the midst of turmoil. By contrast, a still, calm lake may appear so flat that its very stillness belies any possibility of activity. Under that deceptive surface the waters swirl in their own hidden patterns. Of people, too, we speak of 'hidden depths' and 'still waters running deep'.

Watching other people to guess their patterns of thinking takes time and skill. It is all too easy to be led in the wrong direction by taking first impressions as truth. It takes some patience to collect the information that will reveal how an individual really thinks. Since you can't expect your friends and colleagues to have read this book or done the questionnaires, you'll need other ways and means for making their thinking style apparent. What can you do?

The first and most obvious is by observation – particularly by 'listening'. People are telling us all the time about how they think by the way they say things, the words and phrases that are features of their vocabularies. Indeed, part of the research work from which the Colours emerged was based on detailed analysis of the phrases that people use every day to convey their intentions.

How to listen? Take a straightforward and simple approach. Listen for the frequently repeated phrases and interpret which Colour they are coming from.

Here are some examples of the phrases to listen for; try to guess which Colour is driving each group.

GROUP 1
(a) 'I wonder if . . .'
(b) 'Maybe it's possible to . . .'
(c) 'Couldn't it be . . .'
(d) 'Let's experiment with . . .'
(e) 'I've a feeling in my gut that . . .'
(f) 'I don't see why we have to . . .'
(g) 'If we changed this aspect of it . . .'
(h) 'What else could we have missed?'
(i) 'What could it not be?'

GROUP 2
(a) 'I believe . . .'
(b) 'Would you like this . . . or that . . .'
(c) 'This . . . is different from . . .'
(d) 'Prove it . . .'
(e) 'I doubt that . . .'
(f) 'The logic of it is . . .'
(g) 'I'd like to examine . . .'
(h) 'I predict . . .'
(i) 'There's no question in my mind . . .'
(j) 'We must take action . . .'

GROUP 3
(a) 'I've made a list of . . .'
(b) 'We must sort these out . . .'
(c) 'Is this part of . . .'
(d) 'Have I understood rightly . . .'
(e) 'Let's get this straight . . .'
(f) 'I have the sense that . . .'
(g) 'Reading between the lines . . .'
(h) 'Please be specific . . .'
(i) 'I thought I heard you say . . .'

Yes, the first group of phrases is driven by Green, the second by Blue and the third by Red. Or do you doubt that? Read on.

Now try spotting whether the phrases above are Hard or Soft. Have a go before looking at the answers below.

ANSWERS

GROUP 1 Green
(a) Soft   (b) Hard   (c) Hard/Soft   (d) Soft   (e) Soft
(f) Hard   (g) Hard   (h) Hard   (i) Hard

GROUP 2 Blue
(a) Soft   (b) Soft   (c) Hard   (d) Hard   (e) Soft/Hard
(f) Hard   (g) Hard   (h) Soft   (i) Hard/Soft   (j) Soft

GROUP 3 Red
(a) Hard   (b) Hard   (c) Soft/Hard   (d) Hard   (e) Hard
(f) Soft   (g) Soft   (h) Hard   (i) Soft/Hard

You can see from these 'Answers' that there is often doubt about whether the Colour is Hard or Soft. You may well have had doubts about accepting our placings in some of the Colours, too. Language is not pure. Words can cloak meaning as well as reveal it, so listening for people's phrases only gives you one indicator of their intentions. Sometimes, however, it can be obvious that someone has a strong bias to a particular Colour. They are likely to have a few choice phrases that they use repeatedly to indicate the leading drive of their mind. A 'prime' example is Mrs Thatcher. While Prime Minister she has been lampooned vividly on TV and radio by impersonators who could convey her style simply by saying, 'And I believe, I believe very deeply, I believe we have to . . .' Her often-repeated phrase denoted conviction politics, which have been her byword – all strong Soft Blue stuff.

Listening for the favourite phrases people use is a simple and direct way to get a first 'feel' of their leading Colours.

LISTENING FOR INTENTIONS BEHIND THE PHRASES

Of course when people are talking and doing things, they do not always 'introduce' their intentions with convenient phrases which show in which direction their minds are driving. Sometimes, judgements based only on uses of language will prove unreliable and we are better off tuning in to the tone of voice. In addition people misuse and abuse language, particularly verbs, with happy abandon. This brings us the richness of our social conversation but it plays havoc with 'dictionary' meanings of phrases and disrupts the chances of getting a good 'read-out' on their Colours. For example, between a husband and wife there are many phrases, said in a particular tone, which convey hidden intentions behind the up-front intention of the phrase itself. When you know someone well you automatically 'read' their meaning. When you don't know them well there can be amusing and disastrous mistakes. Chapter Six takes a look at the mistaken interpretations of people's intentions.

There are some common phrases that frequently switch the overt language of one Colour to the covert language of another. A favourite is 'I wonder if . . .' Viewed straightforwardly, it is a Green phrase, yet everyone can recognize this as an introduction to a Soft Blue intention that is really saying, 'What I want is . . .', for example boss to secretary: 'I wonder if it is possible to make some improvements to the layout of this report.' The boss isn't in Green, he's being diplomatic in Soft Blue.

We do not suit our intentions to language; we bend it to suit our intentions, at home and at work, with friends, enemies, adults and children. So, as guessers of other people's Colours there is always the difficulty that spoken language contains unspoken intentions. While it is valuable to pick up people's phraseology and use it as a guide, it is one guide only.

EXAMPLES

* '*I believe* we can reach our target by May.' (Soft Blue prediction based on determination to make it.)
* '*I believe* we are going to crack the problem.' (Soft Green intuition that the solution is coming through.)
* '*I believe* the competition is cracking up.' (Soft Red perception of impressions gained about competitors.)

* '*Have I understood rightly* that these figures are now complete?' (Hard Red request for Yes or No truth.)
* '*Have I understood rightly* that this glue will not stick properly onto walls as well?' (Hard Green connection from remark that the glue was not sticking properly onto paper – was this the start of 3Ms on-off glue?)
* '*Have I understood rightly* that the brake horse-power is not enough to handle the weight of the vehicle?' (Hard Blue test to check one fact against another.)

We litter our language with so many phrases which overlay the direct communication of our intentions and meanings, that the observation of the phrases people use must be treated as only *one* means of guessing their driving Colours. Of course, it is also true that some people habitually use phrases to mislead understanding of their thinking: 'Words were given so that we might conceal our thoughts.' It therefore becomes necessary to bring in additional methods for identifying thinking styles.

HUNT THE COLOURS

There are several ways to play this game. Here are two suggestions.

One Make an informed guess. Draw on what you actually know of a person to enhance your possibilities of being right, for example the appearance of their office. One that always looks a mess is likely to have a Green occupant. If it always looks orderly and tidy, you may suppose Hard Red is at work. (You should see our offices!) Your guesses focus your attention more specifically on the person and sharpen your observation of them. You begin to pick up all sorts of clues as to whether your first guess is supportable. This is a very good exercise for developing your Hard and Soft Red skills and it works like this: if you deliberately put a particular angle into your perception to bias your view, your looking and listening will be keener and you will be able to accumulate more relevant information about the other person's Colours than if you just blandly watched them.

Example: We guess that a friend, John, is driven by Soft Red. What evidence? We have noticed that he takes an interest in how we dress. He often comments on the colours we choose to mix and match and on the style of our clothes. Because of his interest in the way we present ourselves, we guess him to be leading with Soft Red. We have also noticed that he pays attention to his own attire, and his office is full of ornaments and pictures. We have frequently seen him show interest in advertisement hoardings, although his job is not in any way connected with advertising. This is the sort of evidence we have mustered to give us our clues about John's leading Colour.

If we observe John more closely as if he were Soft Red, we discover that a lot of his behaviour does not fit. We see him more clearly in our mind's eye because we are looking for what is Soft Red and what is not. We recognize for the first time that he often makes suggestions for improving or changing things. When he comments on the advertisement hoardings he thinks up new ways of putting the ideas across. He also makes suggestions for different outfits we might wear. We realize that his Soft Red interest has a strong Hard Green component in it.

At this point we switch our focus on John and ask whether he leads his thinking with Hard Green. The question is: 'What attracts John's attention first? Is it, for example, being amused by the humour in an advertisement and wanting to cap it or interest in how it conveys the impression of the product? If we cannot distinguish between his Green and Red we can at least be clear that his Blue is not up front. That is important. Knowing the Colour that is least liked and least used is as significant as knowing the leading Colour. Obviously, discovering what kind of thinking a person least likes bears significantly on understanding how they tick and how to work alongside them.

Two You can hunt the Colour even more specifically from conversation. Say we wanted to identify whether John leads with Green or Red. What further clues do we look for? Can we be more specific? Here is a suggested approach. People usually respond in conversation with their most favoured Colour first. If a person with a leading Colour in Red is given a Red statement, they will respond with like kind. It is their favourite Colour and they enjoy being in it, so it is unlikely that initially they will move into another Colour. Conversely, if a Green person at the outset is given a Red statement there is a strong likelihood that their response will be in Green. It would probably take some time to cajole them into Red. The same applies when someone is Blue.

If we guess John is Red, we can anticipate the sort of responses he 'ought' to give. We would therefore begin by leading the conversation in Red to see if he responds in like kind, or whether he gives a Blue or Green response, like this:

Red opening: 'I was reading the other day that the number of people dying of heart disease is higher in Britain than any other European country.'

John may respond: 'Isn't it shocking? This government really ought to do something about the state of the nation's health.' This is an opinion about the information and comes from a Soft Blue stance.

By contrast here is a Hard Red response: 'Oh, really? Where did you read that, can you remember?'

A humorous Green response would be: 'I often wonder if it isn't our statisticians that make us iller than other nations.'

If there is a Green riposte to our Red approach, as above, a Green ploy could be played next to see if John responds in like manner:

Green lead in: 'Wouldn't it be fun if for a day the managing director was made to do the office-boy's job and the office boy had a go at being the MD?'

A Green mind would join in: 'Even more fun to swop their pay cheques as well!'

However, this response: 'Oh, you couldn't do that. It would cause far too much upset,' is Soft Blue, unlikely for a Green person who delights in the unconventional.

A response like: 'It would be interesting to find out what the MD learnt from the experience,' is Red, seeing the idea as a reality that could supply some interesting information.

If our line of questioning has thus far confirmed our suspicion that John is Green, we might try a Blue lead-in:

'I don't like the way your department has been handling the xyz papers lately.'

This response: 'Neither do I. Far too much licence and not enough liberty,' might well endorse your suspicions that John is indeed a Green person.

A Red response would be: 'What makes you think that?'

A Blue defensive response would be, 'Come now, that's a bit steep. Your own hands aren't exactly as white as snow.'

Using this strategy of systematic exploration of a person's responses to Red, Green and Blue initiatives gives you a chance to test out your hypothesis about their driving Colour(s). You can then draw a tentative first conclusion and start to operate, cautiously, with your new-found understanding of their thinking style.

This might lead you on to other kinds of clue. For instance, how long they spend on a Colour, and how deep they go in it. You may also find that some people actually hold off their driving force Colour so as to fling it in to best effect as a trump card. Watch for those Soft Blue people who suddenly take charge – from behind!

It's serious fun, this guessing game.

DIRECT QUESTIONING

It is quite possible, of course, to *ask* your friends and colleagues

about their thinking style – and then help them to think about
how they think.

Mary: 'I'm having some fun investigating thinking styles. I
  wonder what yours is.'

Michael: 'I'm good at maths.'

Mary: 'How come?'

Michael: 'I like handling numbers. They just come naturally
  to me. I like getting answers absolutely right. It feels so good
  to know the answer is the answer and that's an end to it.'

Mary: 'What's so upsetting not getting absolutely right
  answers?'

Michael: 'Oh, the dilemmas – not being sure what's right or
  wrong. I hate being in doubt about things. I like things
  clear-cut and straightforward.'

Even with just a short conversation like this a lot can be
gleaned about Michael's thinking style. What stands out is his
preference for Hard Blue and Hard Red. To be successful
through direct questioning like this requires a skilful Red
approach. For those whose jobs involve professional interviewing and counselling these skills are second nature, but most of
us will have difficulty keeping to the Red thread. Especially
since repeated Red questioning gets to sound like an interroga-
tion. Of course, in formal interviewing questions are expected
and accepted, but if you want to take this approach with friends
or family you probably need to turn it into a game so you have
permission to question them.

Checking Your Own Thinking Style

Of course the methods suggested for guessing other people's
styles can just as appropriately be used on yourself. Although
you have the questionnaires in this book, you may also like to do
some self-observation to cross-check the results. Their authenticity rests on how much truth you could muster about your

preferences at the time. Some quick estimates might have been off the mark. So try another way to pin your thinking style down more accurately.

First, listen for the phrases you commonly use, in particular the ones you often repeat to reinforce your intentions. For example, some people are very fond of using the word 'really', to convey their heartfelt desire to be entirely honest and factual – to be Red. Do you use 'I bet' a lot as a Soft Blue intention? What about the phrase 'let's put it to the test' for Hard Blue?

Secondly, you can play Hunt the Colour on yourself. Pretend that you lead with one Colour in particular. This will give you a focus from which to observe yourself to see how often it drives your thinking. Playing this game is especially interesting if you pretend you lead with the Colour *least* likely to be the one you drive with. By reversing your expectations you come up with some surprising discoveries, which can shake deeply held convictions.

Thirdly, you can conduct an enquiry into yourself by direct questioning. Rope in a friend to play the part of questioner, so that you can be free to explore your own experience. Or you can carry out a scripted paper exercise with yourself. First, list a wide range of your typical activities. They could include things done at home, such as D.I.Y. or writing Christmas cards; or things done at work, such as running meetings, writing reports, dealing with urgent problems, and so on. Be as specific as you can without wasting time. Here is a layout to follow:

* List six activities you most like doing
* List six activities you most dislike doing
* List six activities you are best at
* List six activities you know you do not do well

If you now Colour each activity by rough guessing, it will cause you to work out which Colour is dominant in each activity. The Colour depends on how *you* see it. Each activity could be tackled through any one of the Colours – the question is, which one do *you* use?

EXAMPLES

* An activity like 'tapestry-work' would depend on whether you buy them pre-printed with the colour scheme pre-planned. Then yours would be a Red approach. If you design the patterns and the colour combinations from scratch then you would have a Green approach.

* An activity like 'drafting reports' might be driven by Hard Blue if you see drafting as pulling together the information into a well-thought-out argument. If drafting means generating the ideas for the report, that would be Green. It may be that different aspects of drafting fall into different categories for you. Drafting for logical format may be a least-liked activity and drafting to generate ideas may be something you are good at. You may also like it.

If the activities you chose were not easy to Colour, take more specific aspects of them and then you'll easily be able to see what Colour they are. Every physical activity is also a thinking activity once you go in deep enough. 'Winning a race is all in the mind.' (Daley Thompson, World Decathlon Champion)

These examples show that the way you Colour the activity indicates the way you do it and the way you see the meaning of it for yourself. This provides a vivid picture of what you do well and what badly, what you like and dislike.

You could use blue, red and green highlighters to mark the Colours on the list of activities to give an immediate visual impact. When done, assess your order of preferences under each heading.

* Do some colours cluster at the top of your lists and some at the bottom?

* Do the clusters indicate which Colour is favourite?

* Which is least liked?

* Compare likes and dislikes with what you are best and worst at. Is your best the same Colour as your most liked? (It isn't always.)

* Does this reaffirm what you think is your driving Colour?

* What if the Colour of your 'most liked' is different from what you are 'good at'? Does this show that you have trained yourself well, that you have overcome the bias of your preference, so that you can perform well in a Colour that is not a natural preference?

* Has such a discrepancy between what you like and what you are good at caused you some confusion in the way you understood your own thinking style?

These are questions for which you may not have a ready answer but upon which you may ponder as you consider and reconsider the patterns in your thinking Colours.

CHAPTER SIX

Colour Prejudice

In this chapter and the next we will look at how relationships can be illumined by the Colours. Obviously a subject as broad as 'relationships' could fill a book many times over, so for practical purposes we have to contain our investigation. Use this as a reference chapter, picking out combinations of Colours in relationships that particularly interest you. This is what we zoom in on:

* How people with similar or different driving Colours affect one another
* The problems of mixing them
* How to get the best out of people with driving Colours different from your own
* The impact of Colour differences on teamwork

First let us take a look at some themes which are interwoven into all these issues.

Perception The thread we weave through it all is 'perception'. Relationships are strongly influenced by our perceptions. How people look at one another determines both how they behave together and how they interpret what is said and done. The fascination and fun, the misery and misunderstandings of relationships arise through the struggle to marry our perceptions about others with their own reality and perception of themselves, and vice versa. When your Intention is different from their Perception, who is to say which is the more valid or important? The Colours are a stable lens through which to focus your gaze consciously on others. They also reveal the lenses which others use unconsciously to focus on you.

Task and Person Another theme, central to the Colours, is that it is necessary to view a relationship within a two-fold context: the *purpose* of the relationship, and the immediate *task* which is being done. We form relationships to do things together. Sometimes this purposefulness is forgotten: 'sensitivity' training in the seventies and some 'assertiveness' training in the eighties have tended to focus on the 'relating', losing sight of the realities of the task. Many a bewildered manager has returned from a training course full of 'relating' but unable to relate 'relating' to specific activities and jobs. The Colours, by their nature, enable us to look at all three: the people, their purpose and their task at the same time and through the same perspective.

Integrity The recognition of the integrity of the other person is another theme. It is a fundamental tenet of the Colour Model that when someone is thinking, they seek and strive to 'do the right thing, right'. This is not supposed to be a pious assertion: we are simply saying that nobody actually aims to be stupid. We often do the wrong thing or do something badly, but this is usually because of human fallibility, not by design or intention. When you want to find out how someone ticks, for whatever reason, for example to collaborate better with them or to resolve an antipathy between you, it is necessary to accept that they act from a position of integrity. They do what they think is 'right'. This is such an important point that it is worth elaborating.

'The end justifies the means.' Morally, this may be extremely contentious, but it does illustrate something about intention. Understanding intention is vital to human relationships, which are bedevilled so often by observing only the outcomes, instead of understanding the intentions that drove them. When I do something 'bad', it's because the end I am seeking is 'good'. Just think of examples of this.

* When someone gambles their last pennies it is because *this* time he will be the lucky one.

* When a salesman does another company's product down, it's because he is protecting his own company's interests.

* When the doctor withholds information from dying patients it's for their peace of mind.

* Robbing Peter to pay Paul made Robin Hood a famous hero, not a notorious brigand.

As human beings we may lack the knowledge, wisdom or imagination to do things better but however misguided we may be, our intentions reflect our integrity much more than the outcomes. It is interesting that when someone behaves peculiarly, they are said to be 'out of their mind'.

These then are the themes that infuse these next chapters: perceptions, the context of purpose and task, and the recognition of a person's integrity.

Relationships are based on how we perceive one another, so now we will take a closer look through the Colours at what is meant by 'perceptions'.

Perceptions: Red? Green? Blue?

'He's a very perceptive person!' is quite a compliment. When people say this they are expressing their surprise, delight, or wonder, that the person has revealed what was previously hidden. They recognize what has been brought to light as in some way true. What Colour is perception?

RED

A strict dictionary definition puts perception in Red: 'The absorption and observation of the world about us and inside ourselves through any or all of the physical sensing faculties of the human body'; the active receiving of information, through sight, hearing, taste, touch, smell, warmth, pain, kinaesthetics (sense of movement). When you dance, for example, your perception is actively sending signals from your joints, through your reflexes to your brain in order to ensure you stay upright in relation to the ground. This happens fairly automatically. We are unaware that it's going on, unless we focus on it. So when someone notices something which our own senses are not keen enough to detect, we call them 'perceptive'.

For example, a friend spots a dot on the horizon at sea, which he points out as a ship, when we haven't seen anything. Or a nature-lover 'hears' a noise which passed us by and says, 'That's a hedgehog moving in the bushes.' Or a gourmet friend detects a flavour in a cheese or wine that has eluded our tastebuds. This is a Red kind of perception – and it seems more Hard than Soft because it is the straight observation of physical reality.

Of course, our senses extend beyond the physical. We absorb the world around us and make sense of our inner world, through non-physical senses, which we can describe as Soft Red. These non-physical senses, sometimes called the higher senses, absorb and observe at a deeper reality than the physical. 'A very perceptive person' in Soft Red, is someone whose antennae are pricked to pick up the atmosphere and innuendo that convey the truth behind appearances. For example, an alert Soft Red perceptiveness would 'notice' that a bright cheery smile was hiding sadness. The human mind can divine what is a true reality beyond the outward signs and personal bias. It might be argued that grasping a true reality is beyond human capacity, but remember that the Colours are about intentions. So someone is in Soft Red when they intend either to convey or to tune in to information that is implicit, beneath the surface.

This capacity is much called upon in our relationships with one another, for we hide and cloak our real selves, while needing and longing for our private reality to be perceived. The formal business and commercial world and the Establishment are based on the adoption of roles which overlay our 'real' selves. These disguises serve some valuable purposes – the judge in chambers, the policeman at a riot, the surgeon in the operating theatre, the solicitor in the divorce court. They also cause people to behave 'out of character', inhumanly, without heart, even stupidly. How welcome, then, is the ability to look through the uniform to the human face, the inner torment, the private agony, the personal fears.

GREEN

It is common to accept non-physical 'perceptions' of quite other kinds than Soft Red. We say that someone is very perceptive when they give us a glimpse of another reality, one which requires a leap of imagination and which heralds a vision of something that only might come into being. These are Soft Green prophecies; sometimes we believe them and sometimes we reject them. H. G. Wells, writing at the beginning of the century, foresaw that 'many Londoners in the future may abandon the city office altogether to do their business in more agreeable surroundings'. This is now coming true. Science fiction and the novel are full of such visions. A perceptive person in Soft Green thrills and excites and warns by his insights and even inspires action to make future possibilities a living reality.

Perceptiveness also comes in a Hard Green guise. Here it is to do with the clever twisting of 'normal' Red perception, a distortion of the straightforward view, to generate a new perspective on an old theme. Start-up businesses are usually founded on this kind of recognition of such a new twist. One small business was begun with the idea of refurbishing used metal components by spraying techniques. When the demand for this service fell off, the owner actively engaged his Hard Green mind to think of new outlets. As he searched for possibilities, a series of coincidences affected his perceptions so that he had a breakthrough in his thinking. He came up with the idea of adapting the spraying techniques to prolong the life of new products which are liable to suffer corrosion. 'How perceptive to see such a possibility!' – and quite a different kind of perception from the Soft Green.

BLUE

What of Blue? Yes, we can distinguish both Hard and Soft. In fact, 'distinguishing' is itself Hard Blue perception. When we look to perceive the pattern in things, we use our Hard Blue. For example, faced with a complex problem with conflicting demands from different people, one of the ways to resolve things is by making various comparisons. Finding similarities between some elements and discerning what it is that distinguishes them can be a key step in clarifying a confused issue. It calls upon our rational thinking. When you get through to a simple format, say in a long-lasting negotiation, people say, 'How perceptive!' This is a different use of the mind from the Soft Red perception. Both seem to strive after what is hidden, but Soft Red perceives through a holistic sensing, extracting more from the 'live' experience than a merely literal reading of the situation would seem to justify. Hard Blue perceives through a clear rationality, putting the disinterested Red information to work, arranging the facts into patterns in order to see the logical relationships connecting them.

Soft Blue is another kettle of fish. Oh dear, the difficulties we have here! In fact, the Soft Colours are by no means 'soft options' or an easy way out, but rather more difficult than the Hard because they are more subjective and personal. They offer more scope and therefore more room for error.

When someone backs their own judgement, they are taking a risk from Soft Blue. Some decisions cannot wait for the information that will prepare an adequately Hard Blue cast-iron case. Sometimes you've got all the Hard Blue analysis you can muster, but your decision still rests on Soft Blue faith. As an example, let's take the general manager of a small firm called Zanos, which has just won an unusually large export order. The manager has to choose between a number of different suppliers to meet this order. He interviews, visits and tries to assess (in Hard Blue) their different merits and disadvantages. But all the Hard facts he has to go on are based on the present and the past. He must make his own (Soft Blue) assessments about their performance in the future. He calls on his personal judgement to interpret what they have done in the past to predict for the future. When he boils it all down to the few that meet his absolute requirements, there is so little to choose between Firm A and Firm B that he makes his choice based on his sense of confidence in the M.D. of Firm A.

Months go by, and Firm A provides a satisfactory and helpful service. Firm B goes bust. 'How perceptive he is!' the staff of Zanos remark of their manager. What they mean is, 'How astute he was to pick the successful firm rather than the unsuccessful.' Indeed he was astute. As it turned out his confidence was well founded, although he could not know it at the time.

The Problems of Mixing Thinking Styles

HARD V. SOFT

The complexity of people's perceptions through different Colours affects their relationships. They perceive themselves and one another principally through the Colour that dominates in their thinking style. It is as if they permanently wear spectacles of the hue of their leading Colour.

When two people are together they operate with four perceptual fields between them (at least). (See Figure 6.1.)

6.1

Now let's put the Colours into this interaction. We'll begin with the first major rule:

Hard v. Soft is the Great Divide between people.

We see this at work especially between people whose strong driving Colour is the same but who come from the opposite bias in it. You might think that two such would get along, having in common the same leading Colour. But the power of the Hard/ Soft Divide causes them to see each other with jaundiced eyes. Let's suppose two people are driving Blue thinkers, one from Soft and the other from Hard. Figure 6.2 shows the kind of unpleasant twist they can get into with one another. There are so many variations of this kind of confrontation which we will explore, we have given the syndrome a name: 'j'accuse'. Some are illustrated for you to colour and you could make your own pictures for those that are not. Watch out, though, as the changes in relationships may not be so obvious as they appear.

6.2

Hard Blue   Soft Blue

J'ACCUSE IN THE SAME COLOUR

Blue

Figure 6.2 could suggest to you a familiar stereotype – boss (Hard Blue) and secretary (Soft Blue) relationship, or husband (HB) wife (SB). He prides himself on his rational thinking processes and finds her enthusiasms illogical and unsound. He perceives her to be swayed by her feelings, which annoys him. He thinks she should base her judgements on reason and not emotions. She, on the other hand, senses her integrity to be bound up with her feelings. Her own 'soundness' lies in being able to act in accordance with what she holds dear. She does not require rational argument if she believes something to be right. She thinks he takes needless trouble deciding whether or not to do something when to her the choice is obvious. And when she disagrees with his choice, she gets upset because she feels by her standards that he has contravened important values.

Red

Another stereotype relationship (Figure 6.3) is an accountant (Hard Red) with a salesman (Soft Red). The accountant puts his integrity in accuracy without opinion. The ledgers must

6.3

balance and all regulations must be complied with to the letter (if not the spirit). When he deals with the saleman's monthly expenses he is aggravated by inaccuracies and loss of receipts. This is unreliability, as he sees it, even though the salesman may be the most punctilious keeper of appointments with prospects. The salesman, beleaguered by what he sees as the accountant's petty niggling, thinks the accountant should take a leaf from his book and learn to treat people as human beings instead of form-filling robots.

Green

Two Green characters would never actually clash as the Blues and Reds do, since their energy is not 'people' focused. They both have recourse to worlds of ideas, where people are literally not essential to the main thrust of their thinking. They each pursue ideas in their own way, hardly bothered by the other's *modus vivendi*. For example, if two green types happened to work in the same graphics office on comparable design projects, they would not impinge on one another. The Hard Green fellow would get down to producing many variations on several themes, each repetition having a new twist which stimulates him with further possibilities. The production of examples increases the fertility of his mind. The Soft Green man might go for a walk, have a drink, play through some tapes, read poetry and wait to be 'struck' with the idea. Doing anything definite would curtail his imagination, which he keeps open for inspiration to flow into him. Hard Green sees his colleague as a lucky old so-and-so, who gets ideas just by wasting time doing nothing. Soft Green has a touch of disdain towards Hard Green's industriousness, although he would genuinely admire the result of his colleague's work when he turned in something original.

These examples show that prejudiced perceptions arise between people crossed through Hard and Soft but of the same Colour. The lenses of their own dominant driving Colours twist out of focus the other person's intentions, which are coming from a diametrically opposite pole, even though they are in the same Colour. What happens when people are not only at opposite poles, in Hard and Soft, but also in different Colours? Here are a few examples.

J'ACCUSE BETWEEN THE COLOURS

We have seen the dynamics of a relationship between two

people clashing between Soft and Hard in the same Colour. When we look at Hard versus Soft in different Colours, we discover that not only do people's perceptions of others change as the Colour changes, but what is more significant, their perceptions of themselves are changed by the other person's leading Colour. They feel differently about themselves. It might even seem to someone else that they *are* different.

Look at the changes, for example, in the self-perceptions of Soft Blue when put with Hard Green (Figure 6.4) compared with Soft Blue's self-perception in relation to Hard Blue (Figure 6.2). Notice also the difference in the way Soft Blue is seen by Hard Blue (Figure 6.2) and by Hard Green (Figure 6.4).

6.4

Let's imagine a small business owned by a husband and wife team, Peter (Hard Blue) and Teresa (Soft Blue). Within the dynamics of their Hard and Soft relationship in Blue, Teresa feels her energetic enthusiasm heightened by the contrast of Peter's cool rationality. Recently they have been joined by a designer, John, who is Hard Green. Seeing John's enthusiastic approach to ideas (Hard Green), Teresa initially thought she was dealing with someone like herself. His enthusiasm sparked hers. But in fact, it is different from hers. John is enthusiastic and energetic but only to have ideas and generate possibilities. Teresa now painfully discovers the nature of this enthusiasm (Figure 6.4).

She starts to get impatient with John. Her Soft Blue is eager for action. To her, ideas are not action. She is somewhat phased by the volume of suggestions that John churns out, most of which to her mind are irrelevant. She tries to slice her way into the morass, throwing out what she does not like. She starts treating John with some contempt since she feels he wastes her time when he could have sorted out a good idea before coming to her. This causes him to feel she is constricting his creativity. He is convinced by her heavy-handed rejection of his ideas that she is failing to appreciate all the openings that he is bringing in. He gathers up his ideas from her destructive hands and sees in them a multitude of missed opportunities. All they needed, he thinks, was a bit of development and they could have opened up all sorts of new possibilities.

6.5

Soft Blue Teresa working with her Hard Red accountant becomes a different person (Figure 6.5). His plodding thoroughness in details, amassing facts and yet more facts, makes her feel that her readiness to go ahead and do something without waiting for all the information is positively adventurous. 'How on earth would the business run,' she thinks, 'if we all sat around getting information together and never did anything? We must act, or we'll miss the boat.' The slowness of the accountant's progress when nothing seems to be happening, makes her feel that *her* approach is far more effective. His figure-work and information-gathering is not 'real' work to her. She chivvies him to get on with it. He is dismayed at her haste. His approach is always to find out first and act only when he 'knows'. He feels himself as 'keeper of the integrity' of the project. He fears that if they follow the owner-wife's drive, they will be in danger of making a disastrously wrong decision. He sees his role as ensuring the success of any project by getting the complete picture before a decision to go ahead is made.

We see here the accountant's sense of integrity is bound up with his drive to ensure that the pursuit of Red information is not compromised. This is *his* sense of integrity. Compare this with Teresa's. Hers is bound up with her belief that integrity lies in committing to the action that you believe in. (See Figure 6.2.) She thinks that dithering around compromises the chances of success.

Imagine a large electronics company where a Soft Green research boffin, Colin, finds himself seconded to a project to work with a manager, Janice, who is Hard Blue (Figure 6.6). How would their relationship develop? Being Soft Green he needs to occupy himself with 'irrelevant' activities to allow his ideas to germinate and percolate through to his consciousness. Janice drives for relevance and hard logic. In project meetings, Janice's tightly structured approach makes Colin feel as if he has a noose around his neck, choking his thinking at source. The harder Janice pushes to 'bring him into the discussions', the more he retreats. If he should offer one of his leaps of mind Janice may quosh it immediately with 'Let's keep to the point'. No wonder the two end up with negative perspectives of themselves and each other.

6.6

Claudette (Hard Green) is senior lecturer in the physics department of a university. She drives for ideas, regardless of how other people are feeling and what else they might want to do. Her Soft Red professor, Robin, is eaten up by her voracious Hard Green which plunders his impressions-rich mind for

6.7

ideas and consumes his sensitive energy for support. Claudette gets a lot out of it without realizing what she is doing to Robin. She is just so pleased that her creative output soars when she's with this Soft Red guy (Figure 6.7).

QUICK SUMMARY: 'HARD V. SOFT IS THE GREAT DIVIDE'

The examples on Hard v. Soft are not exhaustive by any means. A careful examination of the examples shows that one or other of the Colours is tending to 'drive' the relationship. Who leads, who follows, who takes and who gives, who tells, and who listens is a function of the individuals' strength of mind. Take the last example of Claudette (Hard Green) and Robin (Soft Red). In spite of the status differences between them, clearly Claudette is the driving personality. She gets what she wants out of their meetings. Perhaps Robin wants to give what he does because he sees how productive she is, but it leaves him feeling drained. If his Soft Red personality drove the relationship, it might look like this:

6.8

Now the boot is on the other foot – so Claudette comes off the worse for wear.

Good Combinations

We have been looking only at the driving Colours, as if the people described had only one Colour. Of course this is unreal, but it demonstrates the power of habitual, dominant leading Colours and how they produce a bind between two people that fixes them, if they are not alive to it, in j'accuse positions. The starkness of such conflict between Hard and Soft is moderated by the interweaving of all the other Colours. Indeed, it is by calling on our other Colours that we can get out of just such a j'accuse bind. Then what is in conflict can be brought into a synergy which is greater than the sum of the two parts. You can always get along with anybody as long as you understand how they perceive you, how you perceive them, and how to go about making the synergy between you. This is covered in the following chapter.

LIKE LIKES LIKE

As you might surmise from the rule 'Hard v. Soft is the Great Divide' the opposite is true: 'Like likes Like', up to a point. We might deduce that all the Softs will enjoy collaborating together and all the Hards. This is so, but there are anomalies. Affinity is natural between two people in the same Mode and Colour, for example two Hard Blues will get on like a house on fire. When it comes to mixing Colours it is not quite so straightforward. Here Red has a special part to play, forming what we call a Utility relationship, for example Hard Red with Hard Blue, or Soft Red with Soft Green. Utilities are so called because Red is utilized to serve the needs of Blue and Green. Then there are the Anomalies, where in spite of the same Mode being up front there is a j'accuse clash.

AFFINITIES

* Hard Blue with Hard Blue
* Hard Red with Hard Red
* Soft Red with Soft Red

* Hard Green with Hard Green
* Soft Green with Soft Green

(Note that Soft Blue with Soft Blue is missing from here)

UTILITIES

* Hard Red with Hard Blue
* Hard Red with Hard Green
* Soft Red with Soft Green
* Soft Red with Soft Blue

ANOMALIES

* Hard Blue with Hard Green
* Soft Blue with Soft Blue
* Soft Blue with Soft Green

It seems to be stating the obvious to say that two people who have the same leading Colours in their thinking style will find it easy to get along together. Yet this 'ain't necessarily so'. In fact when it isn't, the consequences can be especially severe. So let's look at some illustrations, to grasp where Affinities work.

AFFINITY IN HARD BLUE: *Mirrored Reflection: Logic, Soundness and Reason*

What we see here is the happy resonance between two people who can each recognize the way the other person's mind ticks. They reflect one another's perception . . . mirrored reflection. The Affinity is born out of the recognition that they are like each other.

AFFINITY IN HARD GREEN: *Mirrored Reflection: Stimulating and Fun*

Tom and Reg work in a Tax Office. The work is routine and undemanding. They sit opposite each other and to keep their spirits up through the long dreary days, they invent stories based on the papers they are processing. If Tom starts, Reg will pick his story up and weave his own fabrications, bringing in new personalities from the paperwork on his desk. Tom replies in like kind. Their proud record has been to keep one story alive for two months, threading a wildly improbable fantasy from day to day. They increase their amusement by getting their characters into impossible jams and then handing over for the other to find a way out. They rate one another's performance in chocolate biscuits that must be paid at tea and coffee time. (If you are very Blue, this anecdote might make you feel quite indignant!)

AFFINITY IN HARD RED: *Mirrored Reflection: Accuracy, Thoroughness and Order*

Two friends, Jane and Margaret both Hard Red, each have an absorbing hobby. Jane makes tapestries and embroideries. Margaret collects porcelain. In Jane, Margaret has a friend who will happily listen and ask questions about each new item she finds. The relationship is reciprocal. Margaret enjoys examining Jane's work, hearing about the matching of silks, the planning of patterns, the selection of the themes and pictures. It does not matter that their hobbies are different. Their interest and motivation is in accurate, comprehensive information that has time for the fine detail. (If you have a very Blue thinking style you may think this sounds boring!)

AFFINITY IN SOFT RED: *Mirrored Reflection: Receptive Sensitivity, Attunement, Appropriateness*

Gerald and Joe are GPs in a joint Practice. It is a thriving centre, where patients are pleased to see either of them because both doctors give the same kind of attentive care, receptive listening and counselling. Gerald and Joe have built the partnership based on their common appreciation of the 'bedside' manner which they consider to be the lost art of modern medical approaches.

AFFINITY IN SOFT GREEN: *Mirrored Reflection: Intuitive and Imaginative*

Helen and Philippa spend hours in each other's company. They relate endless dreams of what they might be or do one day, with artless disregard for the practicalities. It's as if they share their own mysterious, secret valley, knowing one another's stories, yet not caring in the least if it changes dramatically.

UTILITIES

In the Utilities the Colours feed one another. 'We're a good team' expresses this experience, when people with different capacities quite naturally work well together. Although their minds have different Colour energies, their Mode unites them. They are able to co-ordinate the push of one with the pull of the other to get work done better. Red is the common factor, with its mediating power. You could almost see Red as a ladder reaching to the heavenly ideas people strive for (Green) so that they can be brought down to the ground of judgement (Blue). This middle position represents something very special in the quality of Redness, that is Truth. Truth is neutral. Everything comes to rest in Truth. Judgements (Blue) are no longer necessary when we know. We only have to judge when we *don't* know – indeed, if we actually know, judgement is impossible. Ideas (Green) find fulfilment when they come true. The idea is then no longer a fiction of the imagination, but a fact of life. In a sense Green and Blue seek Red to complete themselves. They always benefit from having some Red around.

THE HARD UTILITIES

Sharon, Hard Red, and Nick, Hard Blue, are both aspiring management trainees with a major clearing bank on their first in-company course. For many of the training exercises they sought each other out because they found they could get the work done effectively together. Some pairings they tried with other members of the course seemed to require a lot of discussion to sort out how to tackle an exercise, whereas Sharon and Nick found they slipped into a give-and-take productiveness as if they had been working colleagues for years.

These Utility perceptions can equally well be applied between Hard Red and Hard Green. There is nothing wildly exciting in these interactions. They are valuable working partnerships which every team needs so that solid results ensue. You will get more effective work from a combination of Hard Blue and Hard Red than from two Hard Blue people. Similarly, Hard Red and Hard Green are more effective than two Hard Green people. In practice, therefore, a team with a job that requires you to tackle the Hard side of thinking should always have a strong Hard Red element in it.

THE SOFT UTILITIES

Turning to the Soft Modes, perceptions here are different from Hard. The Utility relationship operates with a more 'social' face. In the Hard Modes there is a more overtly 'utilitarian' quality in the thinking. Sensitivity about other people is not a priority for the Hard Red mind which wants to get the information regardless. In contrast, the mediator of Soft Red strives to be a sensitive communicator. We can expect this to play a significant part in the relationships with Soft Blue and Soft Green.

Alex, Soft Red, and Krystal, Soft Blue, are young Civil Servants. They have met from time to time at committees and quite spontaneously fall into enjoyable conversation. When Krystal found herself wrestling with an intractable problem she therefore thought of raising it with Alex. Although their meetings had been brief she felt that what they had exchanged revealed a natural trust and understanding between them. When she sounded him out, his feelings were the same. Let's just point out that to Alex's Red mind, 'understand' means 'recognizing what is', in contrast to Krystal's Blue sense that it means agreeing with her. Here is the one slippery feature between them. If Krystal expects Alex to support her in the way she chooses to handle her problem, she might be disappointed. That he understands what she thinks, and why, may not mean that he agrees.

The Soft Utility syndrome is repeated between Red and Green. When Soft Green meets with Soft Red they find mutual interest and understanding. But if Soft Green were to imagine that Soft Red is actually having the same thoughts it would be a mistake. Soft Red looks and listens to Soft Green and Soft Blue with the same ear and eye, not looking for agreement with them, only dispassionate understanding. With sensitivity Soft Red creates the atmosphere of appreciative listening, weaving space to get his message across too. No wonder that Soft Red is seen as a strong card in good salespeople, teachers, journalists, interviewers, counsellors.

ANOMALIES

All three anomalies involve Blue, the Colour of judgement. Judgement cuts, decides, divides. It says 'yes' to this and 'no' to that, splitting the sheep from the goats. The divisive nature of Blue is always likely to cause dissension, for whenever a decision is taken in favour of one thing it means that all others are rejected. Someone is bound to be upset. Anyone using Blue needs to be highly aware of its divisiveness. Blue's convergence is quite distinct from Red's mediation and Green's fertility. Red mediates conflict through truth and Green escapes conflict through new ideas which get around the difficulty by ingenuity and imagination. Conflict is created by Blue.

Hard Blue with Hard Green Yes, we are back with j'accuse once more. These two really have a difficult time together. Their intentions drive in totally different directions and without a bridge of Red between them they cannot work together. Hard Green's thinking proliferates with angles, swings, jumps, dives, and runs, in relentless pursuit of yet another thought which will make something different, better, quicker or simpler. Hard Blue moves on narrow paths, on prescribed routes through known territory. If it skips a step it fears it will make a mistake, create faulty logic, ruin the result.

Ken and his wife Dorothy are seeking a divorce. Their marriage is breaking down because they just cannot get along in the practical matters of family life. Ken's Hard Blue cannot adapt to his wife's Hard Green life-style, which he feels inflicts a home-life on him that is intolerably disorganized. Dorothy never finishes anything and is never on time. Meals are always late, the children up till all hours, the house always a tip. What had been an attractive vivacity in courtship became an intolerable chore in marriage. For her part, Dorothy is deeply disappointed in her husband. She had expected him to cut a dash in life, to create openings in business and in their social life which would bring her scope for her exploratory energies. Ken's demands for a settled life-style are killing her spirit.

Soft Blue with Soft Blue Now, why should these be Anomalies? Aren't these two both striving towards the same result, coming to judgement? You'd think that would unite them in a unity of purpose and process. The catch lies in the Data. If both have the *same* Data in their opinions, values, predictions and interpretations, their Process will harmonize with great ease. But if their Data is *different* they could be into authentic conflict.

There is almost a quality of conspiracy when people discover that they like to get things done under the same framework of belief. Take an example of two people who both believe in trade unionism. Foreman Bill, strong in Soft Blue, often has to deal with his shop-steward, Andy, also strong Soft Blue. They both like to get a decision made without too much humming and ha-ing. One might imagine that being on different sides of the management fence, they would be on a collision course for frequent industrial conflict. Not so. Both men, not just Andy, are firm union supporters. Bill comes from a family of active trade unionists. His roots lie deep in the movement. Regardless of their job status, a higher common value (the preservation of trade union rights) governs how they deal between themselves on each particular problem.

6.9

What a contrasting situation Bill has with his boss, Mike, who is also a Soft Blue man. Mike is a Liberal. He has no difficulty in respecting his foreman's right to believe and support trade unionism but he is strongly opposed to the enforced regimentation and demarcation practices it results in. The two men have protracted arguments about the way in which the shop-floor should be managed. Mike considers that Bill betrays management responsibilities when he makes agreements that uphold trade union rights which Mike considers to be an infringement of other people's rights. (Figure 6.9, Authentic conflict.)

Authentic Conflict Because both these men are strong in their Soft Blue Process there is no simple way they can find to get around their differences. Both of them think it is important to uphold what they believe in, in all that they do. Their beliefs are central to their way of doing things. They are the types who, during the religious swings of the Reformation, would have died at the stake rather than forswear their faith. Thomas More and Martin Luther, and his namesake Martin Luther King, were men of this powerful ilk. Thousands of people are willing to modify their values when the political climate changes, but not Soft Blue types. When others adapt their perceptions because their sense of their integrity is not bound up with firm adherence to a set of beliefs, Soft Blue people will resign, be sacked, sell everything they own, to protect or clear their good name.

Soft Blue and Soft Green In Process these two have in common a passion for their own Data. If they also share the same Data they will get along very well. While Soft Blue is motivated by its ideals, Soft Green is absorbed by its ideas. Soft Blue leads by the winning power of conviction, the belief that the cause is right. Soft Green, in contrast, leads by the winning power of vision, the dream of a new world. Put these two together and if they find common ground in the content of their beliefs and visions they can move the earth.

Authentic Conflict What if the Data is different? Soft Blue will destroy what it can of the heretical Green ideas. Look at the fuss that is generated when a member of the British Royal family espouses something that is in advance (Green) of the Establishment view, like alternative therapies, vegetarianism, ecological farm management. Newspaper columnists rush into print to decry, ridicule and belittle them. This is Soft Blue reacting, because most newspapers, although they claim to bring us news (Red) actually bring us views (Soft Blue). If the news were really Red, then Green would have impartial coverage and readers would really be able to find out (in Red) about current affairs and make up their own minds (in Blue) on whether they agree with their leaders, or not. As it is, journalists and TV interviewers usually take an angle, take up a position, give the story a slant, not news but views. Isn't it significant that in 1985 a Poll in Britain asked the public to judge various occupations on honesty and ethics? Members of Parliament came out bottom of the list, but journalists were not included in that survey. In 1986 journalists were included and replaced MPs at the bottom of the poll.

Who Is the Real Self?

We have looked at the crossed (and cross!) perceptions between different Colour Modes, as if they only existed within separate individualities. All of them also live within one individual, within one's own mind, yours and mine. The j'accuse conflicts, the Affinities, Utilities and Anomalies are within us. The Colour dynamics which we see operating between people also operate within our own souls. The Hard and Soft Divide out there between people is also in here within me. So please consider this chapter as an analogy of your personal thinking energies. You will appreciate the value of this when you look at Chapter Seven to see how the conflicts can be bridged. By examining how to bridge the gaps between people of different Colours it also gives you clues about how to resolve your own internal conflicts. We all know the trauma of divided thoughts, when one part of your mind seems to pull you one way and another tugs you in an opposite direction. With the language of the Colours and Modes you can now describe to yourself what is going on within. With this language you can understand the 'how' of your intentions pulling you this way and that, so you are in a better position to handle them.

CHAPTER SEVEN

Overcoming Colour Prejudice

This chapter shows how differences of thinking style between people need not produce conflict but can be creatively co-ordinated. Such co-operation is achieved by recognizing and working positively with the other person's style. Although the expressions of our thinking are richly diverse, the deep structures of the Colours are common to all of us. An obvious analogy is in the diversity of everyone's appearance which is based on the universal components of the human physical structure. We all have limbs of muscle and bone which are co-ordinated through a central nervous system. The mind, like the body, has basic components too. Let's stretch the physical analogy a little further. Limbs can be likened to the Colours, Blue, Red and Green; the bones likened to the Hard Mode and muscles to the Soft.

When one Colour swamps an individual's thinking style it can be difficult to appreciate that they also embody all the other Colours in their mind. As Chapter Six showed, two people who allow themselves to be swamped by conflicting intentions have great difficulty in seeing each other's integrity. There are ways open to anyone to break the spell of these imbalances and counter the distortions they inflict on us. This is not to take individuality from thinking. Without that we would all be less creative. Rather, let's look at how diversity can find common ground within the deep structure of the Colours.

Crossing the Great Divide

The previous chapter illustrated how a strong lead in one Colour can preclude someone from appreciating another's very different thinking style. Indeed those differences can annoy, irritate, exasperate or cause anger. This is because we are looking through our own driving Colour, which distorts what we see of theirs. If we could only see them as they see themselves we would discover our differences to be only in Process, not in Data. Process conflict can be resolved by changing your process of thinking. It is within your own control. Unlike Data conflict, which is 'authentic' (see Figure 6.9), j'accuse (process conflict) has no substance. If you broaden your understanding and stretch your capacities of mind, much of what you take to be real disagreement is only 'process' deep. Hard and Soft hold between them a wonderful potential for powerful and abundant synergy if they only get their act together. Let us look at how the canyon that separates them can be bridged.

BUILDING BRIDGES ACROSS J'ACCUSE

The characteristics of the j'accuse syndrome are repetitiveness and impasse. Both sides keep saying the same things over and over again, each driving the other further away into alienation. Each is thrown into a fixed opposing position where all other thinking capacities are submerged under the grip of the two fighting Colours. In extreme cases they can even be at one another's throats, flinging around words like 'Liar!', 'Cheat!', 'Stupid!', when in fact they might not really disagree with one another at all. This is because what people think or say is driven by the Colours they are using at that moment – and neither of them realizes it is the Colours that are doing the clashing of horns. Both sides become single-tracked, locked into driving Colours which exclude other Colours that could come to their rescue. No one is naturally bound to only one

Colour, but a j'accuse relationship with another person can make us appear to be.

Take the example of the Hard Blue husband and the Soft Blue wife. They *anticipate* each other's fixed reactions whatever the issue, new or old, and thereby confirm in one another the oppositions of their leading Colours (Figure 7.1).

7.1
Hard Blue   Soft Blue

Faced with even a small decision they will promote the likelihood of disagreement at the outset with a remark like, 'I know what you will want but I . . .'. They set up the division between themselves by always placing the other into their habitual predominating Colour.

> Step One:
> Breaking the j'accuse mould can only begin when we recognize its symptoms and wish to do something about them.

Since it is all too easy to be swallowed up by the argument and disarray of j'accuse we must learn to take a step backwards from the particulars of the argument in order to perceive just which Colours are driving us. Our research has shown that more disagreements take place through misalliance of the Colours than actual information discrepancies. In other words, the process of thinking is causing the difficulty, not the data. More often than not, people have mismatched their Colours and created a dispute out of the process misalliance rather than real disagreement over data. When the data appears to be at the root of the trouble it is usually because it has been brought into the arena via the conflicting Colours, which create different perceptions about the data.

The Hard Red accountant, Howard, and the Soft Red salesman, Ben, mentioned in the previous chapter were locked into a monthly cycle of irritation (Figure 7.2). Do they ever look beyond the surface irritations? Howard is peeved every time Ben presents incomplete expense sheets. Ben is peeved every time Howard requires better records from him. Both hold the other in low esteem. They are caught by their driving Colours. Now they need to lift their heads from the peevishness of their feelings and move back from the immediacy of the point at issue, in order to examine each other's Colours.

> Step Two:
> Most conflict arises through mis-perception and misunderstanding of one another's thinking intentions. Step back from the argument and look for the Colours that are operating adversely.

As soon as one of the parties in a j'accuse conflict is aware of which Colours between them are at war, a path out of the conflict can be sought. Break the circle physically and mentally. Change your position. Stand up or sit down, walk about, stretch. This physical movement will help you change your thinking position. Step back mentally from the conflict and shift into another Colour.

> Step Three:
> Break the circle. Move yourself and move your mind to find a Colour that will support and harmonize.
> * Join the other person in their Colour, or
> * Move into a Colour that has Affinity with the other's, or
> * Move into a Colour that has Utility with the other's

Any one of these moves will release the tensions and enable both of you to take more sympathetic stances. To choose which move to make depends on what anyone can access within themselves in the given situation. Obviously it is easier to pick a Colour that figures fairly strongly for you rather than going for one for which you have little natural liking or ability. Let's look at several examples to see how these moves can operate.

Example One The accountant, Howard, and the salesman, Ben.

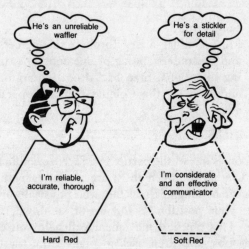

7.2

Hard Red   Soft Red

Howard's thinking style in order of preference	Ben's thinking style in order of preference
1. Hard Red	1. Soft Red
2. Hard Blue	2. Soft Blue
3. Hard Green	3. Hard Blue
4. Soft Blue	4. Soft Green
5. Soft Red	5. Hard Green
6. Soft Green	6. Hard Red

Their 'normal' relationship via the monthly expense returns (so typical a situation for sales people and also 'creative' people like journalists), throws them both into their respective leading Colours, causing them to be aggravated with each other. (Hard Red v. Soft Red.) Given their thinking preferences as listed above, what other Colours could they each call upon to lead them out of the circle of their conflict? Their options are any one of three possible moves:

i) Join the other in their Colour. Realistically this isn't likely! Ben's Hard Red is at the bottom of his pile of thinking preferences. Howard's Soft Red is almost at the bottom. Both of them would have great difficulty moving into the other's leading Colour; accessing it within themselves would mean they have to dig deep into their least used Colours.

ii) Move into an Affinity. There is a real possibility here. Third in the salesman's thinking preferences is Hard Blue. Second in the accountant's list is Hard Blue. If Ben can shift his pitch to Hard Blue he will have an affinity with Howard's Hard Blue. If Howard is attracted by that move so that he shifts into it also, there is a real chance that these two might find a way forward together.

iii) Move into a Utility. This is probably the best move of all. At first sight it might appear to be the same move as the Affinity, but it isn't, because Ben is seeking to find a Utility relationship with Howard's Hard Red without requiring the accountant to shift his Colour at all. Hard Blue can work quite amicably with Hard Red.

How might this work in practice? Let's take the Utility move as the best option, since it requires the least effort from one side of the conflict. Let's suppose that Ben the salesman, being Soft Red and therefore having a basic desire to communicate well with everyone, decides that he must do something to break the petty annoyances of the monthly expenses. He realizes through his Soft Red antennae that the accountant lives in an entirely different world from his own, with different pressures.

Ben draws on his empathy to motivate him to look for a change in their way of handling one another. He acknowledges privately that his own behaviour adds to Howard's pressures just as much as the accountant's behaviour adds to his. He also recognizes that the accountant, who relies on the chits for certification of the expenses incurred, does not trust his honesty. Ben's feeling goes like this: he is the best salesman around; it's only a small company and the orders he brings in are what really matters. He can't be bothered to deal with little bits of paperwork when he's out in the field. He sees his expenses claims as a matter of swings and roundabouts – one month he'll estimate up, the next down. Yet he can see that the accountant has nothing else but chits to rely on. Here the salesman's Soft Red 'feel' for the truth of their respective situations is governing his thinking. He starts to think of the accountant as a prospective client who needs to be understood and worked with instead of a work colleague who should provide him with an expenses service that suits Ben's needs. Maybe Howard should be offering such a service, but at the moment he doesn't see it that way and the company's systems do not promote that attitude either. The accountant, as the guardian of the company's rules, is unlikely to shift his attitude, so the salesman is the one who has to move first.

How does Ben proceed in his thinking process? His Soft Red has given him a clear appreciation of the situation. Now his Soft Blue values come into play. (Soft Blue is his second Colour.) He values being successful in all his dealings with people. He likes people and feels bad about his monthly scraps with Howard. He even feels sorry for the accountant, whose job he considers very limiting. Here is a chance to make someone else's life a bit easier, and his own into the bargain. So he commits himself through his Soft Blue to take some action. Next, he moves into his Hard Blue, his third Colour. He analyses the way he does his expenses. As his Hard Red is low he doesn't do a very good job of it, because he doesn't bring in enough detailed information to make the analysis very rigorous. But at least he tries. He recalls how he often forgets to make up his expenses chits at the end of the day. How often? Well, he isn't sure. Maybe one night in three. Is there any pattern to the way he forgets? (Hard Blue question.) He can't be sure because his memory for the detail of what he actually does is not 'alive' to him; that kind of Hard Red data is lowest on his thinking list.

What practical action could he take to jog his memory each day and ensure that he actually makes out his chits? Could he start some kind of routine which would cause him to complete his chits before he leaves his car? *That* does not appeal to him. He is often so tired that he just wants to relax in his local for a refreshing half-hour before meeting the onslaught of the family. At this point his Soft Green starts coming into play . . . suggesting wonderful pictures of how to resolve the problem . . . a beautiful secretary as his permanent amanuensis . . .

At this point, waking from his dreams with a start, he has another idea (Hard Green). Why not get Howard to give him the solution? If he approaches him in Hard Blue (Utility with Hard Red), there is a possibility of the joint discussion bringing a fruitful outcome. Why not, for example, ask the accountant some Hard Blue testing questions: Why is this level of detail necessary for the system to operate effectively? Why was this system chosen? Why were other systems rejected? Why weren't the people whom the system is supposed to serve ever consulted? Haven't they ever heard of approximation, or a standard amount per diem?

These sorts of questions which ask for the Hard Blue logic of the system will lead the accountant to give lots of Hard Red answers, providing background information, and then also to engage his own Hard Blue to start reviewing the soundness of the system as it stands. His mind is engaged because Ben is interested in the system Howard has to work with daily, and its objectives. They start to get alongside one another in Hard Blue. Howard even begins to reveal how the system does not meet its targets satisfactorily. He confesses his own dissatisfactions with how it runs. How it makes more work for him than is actually necessary. How the forms could be simplified. How the duplication of effort is wasteful. The two men realize that they both suffer under the same system but for different reasons (Soft Blue). They can then begin to look for ways to help one another (Hard Green). The accountant has a store of examples for managing records so he patiently works through them to identify (Hard Blue) one that will enable the salesman to manage his expenses with a minimum of fuss.

This story tells of the kind of triviality with which everyone who belongs to an organization is familiar. It impedes good working relations and attention to effective activity. The solution seems obvious but the will to take a small step like this can be lacking all round. Small things create great waves. The salesman may want to find his fortune elsewhere. His manager may be under pressure to bring him into line or fire him . . . his best man in the field!

Example Two Teresa and John (from Chapter Six). How do their thinking preferences pan out?

Teresa	John
1. Soft Blue	1. Hard Green
2. Soft Red	2. Soft Green
3. Hard Red	3. Soft Red
4. Hard Green	4. Hard Blue
5. Hard Blue	5. Hard Red
6. Soft Green	6. Soft Blue

Their habitual j'accuse stance (Figure 7.3) leads them into a spiral of misunderstandings in their work, as we saw earlier. Teresa wants to get things done. John wants to offer new ways for getting things done. How can they overcome the fundamental cross purposes in their objectives and intentions?

7.3

i) Join the other in their Colour. John would find it difficult to join Teresa since his Soft Blue comes last. Teresa might just be able to make the bridge to John since her Hard Green is fourth.

ii) An Affinity. This has possibilities. Soft Red is second for Teresa and third for John.

iii) The Utility relationship is another possibility. John's Soft Red in third place may work with Teresa's Soft Blue, her leading Colour. Or Teresa's Hard Red at the third position may work with John's Hard Green in number one position.

These options give them lots of scope to rescue themselves from the clashes between their leading Colours. But someone has to move first to break the spell. How could either one make it happen? Teresa's Soft Red is most likely to prompt her to look for better communication between them. The most obvious way is to appeal to John's Soft Red. She decides that the next time he upsets her she will avoid getting annoyed. When she finds herself getting cross yet again with John's tardiness in finishing a project (because he has decided to pursue yet another interesting idea) she sees the look on his face. It's obvious he's feeling crushed. Teresa's Soft Red is sensitive to his state of mind. She catches her anger before she gets too deeply in to the j'accuse spiral with him. She listens to her Soft Red instead of her driving Soft Blue.

From her Soft Red she is able to say, 'Look, I realize you were doing your best to make a good job of this project. Tell me what you saw as the scope of this task and how much freedom you had to stretch time limits.' She is asking him to respond from his Soft Red to her Soft Red enquiry. If he can hear that her intention is to find out and not to scold, John may be able to respond in like manner. If, however, her question still sounds to him like her usual Soft Blue criticisms, he may respond in his usual Hard Green manner. 'There are so many possibilities we haven't pursued yet. I can see at least three chances for us to get one up in the market. We could try an elastic scheduling, we could bring in more staff, we could employ better software. I was wondering if we could increase the budget in order to consider new hardware, too.'

Indirectly, from his Green, he has answered her question, if she has the wit to see it. He felt he had the scope to go on with the project until he got the best idea, and he hasn't come up with it yet. The subtlety of Soft Red should enable Teresa to recognize what he has told her. However he has stayed in Green. If he sticks there Teresa's Soft Red will have to do all the work of understanding. This will re-activi-ate her Soft Blue annoyances and frustrations. She must shift him out of Hard Green. Her first ploy has failed. And she can't be sure if he is hearing her Soft Red. She can try again. 'I do understand that you are looking for the best approach. It's necessary to consider a variety of possibilities. Is that the complete list now?'

John: 'Well, it's never going to be complete. You can always think of another way. For example, I've begun to create some scenarios for ten years time, that will give us far greater insight into new possibilities than we have pursued so far.' (Hard Green)

Teresa's Soft Red is activating another j'accuse dynamic. Instead of moving from his Hard Green, John is lapping up the Soft Red interest and using it to support his own Hard Green process. Her hopes that he would move into his Soft Red have not materialized. Soft Red is too far down his thinking style. Instead of resolving the Blue v. Green conflict she has got them into a Soft Red v. Hard Green j'accuse situation.

Now what? Trying to evoke an Affinity with John through Soft Red has failed. Perhaps she can bring in her Hard Red to provide a Utility combination to take the pressure off and thus lead them into some kind of resolution? Hard Red is third on her list. Her approach might be this:

Teresa: 'Look, show me what you've got worked out on your ideas. Let's take a closer look at the different possibilities (Hard Red). Then we will both be fully in the picture and I'll better appreciate what you're wrestling with' (Soft Red).

John: 'It would be better if you waited until next week when I'll have a lot more to show you on paper. Or I could dictate what I've got in my head to Jessica, or if she is busy I could use the dictaphone.' (Yet more Hard Green.)

Teresa, ignoring this and sticking to Hard Red: 'Well, if we start from what you've got, you can fill in the details verbally and I can take notes.'

John: 'Okay. Where shall we begin?' (At last, a Hard Red response.)

They are both in Hard Red, and able to plough through the information that is essential for them both to grasp the scope of the problem John is facing. Teresa had to work persistently and unselfishly but she made it in the end. This one swallow won't make a summer out of John and Teresa's working partnership. Sometimes the commitment to cross the j'accuse divide has to be sustained over a long period before a new pattern of relationship is developed. That can place a heavy demand on the one who is struggling to build the bridges, until the other starts from their end.

Example Three Bill and Mike (from Chapter Six)

7.4

The divide between Hard and Soft is not the only cause of j'accuse. In Chapter Six we looked at Anomalies and took as an example Bill and Mike, who were both strong in Soft Blue. When two people of the same Mode of the same Colour meet, instead of the Affinity you might expect, there could be rich conflict. One such Anomaly is Soft Blue with Soft Blue. One is tempted to think for example that two Soft Blue people should get on thrillingly well, but they will do so only as long as they value the same things. They will clash when their Soft Blue data differ, their beliefs, their values, their opinions and their predictions (Figure 7.4).

What routes are open to them to resolve such conflicts? How about using the three moves suggested for handling j'accuse a little earlier? Unfortunately these possibilities are rather thin. Soft Blue by its closing nature shuts out many openings. One of the recurring difficulties of Soft Blue is that it converges. A closing strategy is very pertinent when the time is ripe to make a decision, but 'en route' to that moment Soft Blue's tendencies to shut down too soon on alternatives is a handicap. So what moves are available?

i) Obviously to join the other in their Colour is not on since they are both already in the same Colour Mode and also in conflict.

ii) Moving into a Colour with an Affinity is also nullified, because no affinity exists for Soft Blue.

iii) What of the possibility of moving into a Colour with a Utility to the other? Yes, there is one possibility here: Soft Red. Since a Utility relationship uses the mediating power of Red, Soft Blue can be mediated by it. But this can only operate when one or other of the two parties involved is prepared to adopt it. That isn't always possible if the thinking preferences of each of the two parties places Soft Red low on their list.

Both Bill and Mike lead from their Soft Blue. These are their thinking preferences:

Bill	Mike
1. Soft Blue	1. Soft Blue
2. Hard Blue	2. Soft Green
3. Hard Red	3. Hard Green
4. Hard Green	4. Soft Red
5. Soft Red	5. Hard Red
6. Soft Green	6. Hard Blue

It is unlikely that either of these two will be able to access their Soft Red in order to form a Utility with the other's Soft Blue. Frankly, neither of them is likely to be able to dig that deep to resolve this clash without very powerful motivation and some real help to boost their abilities to handle Soft Red. Improving one's ability with low-preference Colour Modes is certainly a positive step towards conflict resolution (see Chapter Eight). But presuming these two have to sort their problem out on their own, what can they do about their deep difference?

This is not an easy issue. The room for manoeuvre is tight. It does throw up the very real phenomenom that when two Soft Blue people meet on opposite sides of a conflict they are heading for a long, maybe bitter, struggle. They will hold onto their different positions like grim death. We have seen much of this between British unions and management. Each negotiating team seems to assume a corporate thinking style driven by Soft Blue. Industrial disputes of this nature are usually resolved by producing what is politely called a face-saving formula. It is composed in such a way that it looks as if both sides maintain their traditional (Soft Blue) standpoints. But neither gets what they really need. They both end up losers in order to preserve what they tenaciously hold dear. When negotiating teams are reduced to dependence on one driving Colour, namely Soft Blue, they will move, but slowly. They need imagination (Green) to suggest other ways around the issues and information (Red) to give more understanding of the other side's position.

The best way forward when two people are locked into this kind of conflict is to generate more room for movement. This can be done in two ways: by bringing in another person with a different leading Colour, and by introducing a 'thinking agenda'.

THE THINKING AGENDA

Taking the second point first, agreed 'thinking agendas' can be used to steer people so that they move into and out of the Colours that are needed to resolve any particular situation. Such an agenda, which we call a Colour-Map, shows what Colour is needed to achieve what kind of outcome. By using it to shape discussion, everyone's thinking style can be kept within some kind of discipline to meet the demands of the task. A Colour-Map is an entirely new concept in the world of management. It enables an individual, a pair or a group to organize their thinking strategies to harmonize both with the task they are doing and with one another.

When two Soft Blue people are locked in conflict they can benefit enormously from thinking agendas. If they can observe the discipline of using one it will act like an outside energy or force, giving them new directions to break the bind of their concern with one another's values. It will lead them into Red and Green as well as Blue. These thinking agendas are invaluable for anyone who is in a j'accuse position. If neither side has the energy of purpose to shift their Colour on their own volition, agreeing to use the same Map could push them out of their impasse, and then serve as an impartial referee.

Colour-Maps are not the only possibility. Bringing in other people with different thinking styles to swell the Colour resources at your disposal, is another way forward. Two Soft Blue types in j'accuse principally need a Red mediator. However, a Green options-creator is also very useful, as long as the mediation has been well established. So the choice and timing for bringing in colleagues to help out is an important issue. It is an issue that is heightened when it comes to building teams who must manage their conflicts from within their own ranks. How do you create a team of people who can satisfactorily provide their own checks and balances against destructive conflict?

USING THE COLOURS FOR TEAMWORK

The word 'team' implies a successful collaboration between people. There is something of a fashionable tendency in business these days to throw intractable problems at a hastily selected group in the mistaken belief that they will automatically generate some special magic and triumphantly see the problem off. Many teams do not thrive. In fact, the fusion of an effective team takes time as well as careful selection. The members must have a good understanding of thinking processes, both as individuals and within the group dynamics. It would be foolish to imagine that the inclusion of a third person in a j'accuse conflict will in itself be the simple remedy. A third person will not turn a warring twosome into a team and certainly will not ensure that conflict is brought to an end.

Our lives are full of teamwork. Almost everyone will have

some experience of this in partnerships – for example, in marriage, in business (secretary and boss), in sporting activities (coach and athlete) or in artistic pursuits (singing teacher and pupil). We have already looked in depth at twosomes to see how the Colour dynamics operate. We have seen some of the clashes that occur. We have also seen the synergies. Larger teams, like the family, the management project group, the departmental section, the interviewing/assessment panel, the audit team, the detective squad, the chamber quartet or the travelling pop group are another kettle of fish. We might well ask, 'When is a team a team?' Is a Board of Directors a team?

Here is a way of describing a team: three or more (but probably not more than eight or ten) people who are actively collaborating to enhance one another's effectiveness to achieve common objectives. Sometimes all its members meet as a team, sometimes just a few. It is a growing, learning body, with a life of its own. Members of the team will also work separately on their common objectives. They should be interested in one another's progress and development as well as in the project or task they have to do together. Perhaps you would like to draw your own conclusions as to whether your Board of Directors can be classified in the team-working category.

A good all-purpose team will include representation of all the Colours and a balance of Hard and Soft. With such a spread of thinking, the group should be able to ensure that no two people in the team ever get stuck in j'accuse. Of course, oppositions will arise, but the two who are in opposition should not be left to struggle alone. The sensitivity of the team to their Colours should enable them to apply the appropriate Colours to release the chains. They can use any one of the three possible moves we looked at in previous examples:

* Join the other person in their Colour, or
* Move into a Colour that has Affinity with the other's, or
* Move into a Colour that has Utility with the other's

Teams sometimes have unbalanced groupings of the Colours among their membership. An audit team, for example, often has Hard Blue- and Hard Red-biased thinkers. This can be very limiting when they are dealing with the personnel of a company they are auditing. The auditors' tendency would be to carry out a narrow definition of their task which cuts out the niceties of human relations of the Soft kind. In the end their zealousness for the Hard hinders the collection of the hard data, since the people they had no time for are the very ones who must provide it. Such an audit team would do well to look to its balance of Hard and Soft in its collective thinking style. It might appear to be counter-productive to include a team member who is less hard-data driven, but actually it would be a wise move. The best audit teams we know always have at least a dash of Green among them, and sometimes it is found in the most senior member.

This points up a real issue in team-building. Not only must the team include the necessary skills and thinking capacities to tackle the task to be done, it must also embrace a breadth of capacity to forestall the dangers of j'accuse. This is a good maxim to apply in recruiting personnel within a small department, where everyone's two-pennyworth counts. It applies equally well for an Apollo space team, the staffing of a small shop, a nursing ward, a chamber quartet, and so on. It takes more than expertise in the task to make a successful team.

SUMMARY

Working relationships are peppered with minor irritations, misunderstandings and petty upsets which are due to the blind mixing of thinking styles. The cocktails of Colours which get shaken and stirred together at work can produce some unpleasant, even disastrous, potions. However, with judicious attention to thinking process and a willingness to look at how it causes conflicts, people can avert head-on collisions. The examples of Teresa and John and the salesman and the accountant, show how individuals with different styles can resolve Colour conflicts between them. When the issue is the rather more intractable matter of Soft Blue values – authentic conflicts – those involved probably need to draw in help from outside themselves in the form of a Colour-Map or a third person who can act as a Red mediator.

Personal integrity is an unseen constant within all un-productive conflict of this kind. No matter whether your fight is with an angry secretary, an overbearing boss, an irritating subordinate, an impossible colleague, a recalcitrant customer, an awkard teenager or an unhappy partner in marriage: when two people are in conflict there is unspoken nastiness around which undermines their respect for the other's integrity. It takes considerable strength of soul to look beyond the bad feelings to the human heart that is seeking to do the right thing in the right way. A willingness to look is the start of conflict resolution.

Then comes the difficult step of taking responsibility for making a real effort to resolve the conflict. Teresa was willing to accept that her thinking style and the way she had handled things had already contributed to the difficulties with John. She took the initiative regardless of who started the conflict or who was the most to blame for its continuation. She wanted to generate a productive relationship; she was willing to try and keep on trying.

The next step is to recognize what is causing the conflict. Usually we look at what has been going wrong to ascribe blame or fault (Soft Blue). But we need to turn our eyes through Red to examine the processes of the interactions. These are the questions to ask:

'How could my way of going about things (my thinking style) mislead them about my intentions?'

'How does their way of going about things (their thinking style) mislead me about their intentions?'

These two questions invite a guess at the other's thinking style (see Chapter Five) so that the mis-match between the two sides can be analysed. List your thinking Colours in order of importance, 1 to 6, side by side with the list of your adversary's, as you have guessed them. The contrasting pattern of the styles should provoke some immediate thoughts about the causes of conflict. Refer also to Chapter Six where the j'accuse conflicts are set out in detail.

This analysis of thinking styles will provide a feel for the roots of the conflict which lie either in the processes of the j'accuse Colours or in the strength of the differences in Soft Blue values. Once you have identified the cause you can make imaginative use of the guidelines in this chapter to find a way forward, always remembering that what you learn about resolving conflict out there will have bearing on how you resolve it in your own mind.

CHAPTER EIGHT

Enriching Your Colours

In this chapter we take a longer-term view of your thinking style. We will look at how to develop your Colours for two purposes: to boost the Colours with which you have least facility, and to enrich the ones for which you have greatest affinity.

GREEN HEALTH WARNING!
Reading this Chapter straight through may lead to mental constipation. It is designed for reference only.

Select what you want, be quite specific about your choices, and focus on them clearly so that you work effectively with them. The opening Sections One and Two will give you a sense of how to get going, what stops you and how to plan your development strategy. The bulk of the rest of the chapter describes exercises for each Colour.

Section One
Getting Going and What Stops You

If you want to improve your skills in handling your Colours, follow the path used for learning things which require development over a period of time, namely, regular exercise. Take athletes as an example. Amateur or professional, they must adopt a programme of regular daily exercises for overall strength, stamina and flexibility and for the particular muscles required for their sport. The exercises are carefully chosen, sequenced, monitored and executed within specific time-frames, outside the pressures of competition. The routines, as part of a system of physical well-being, lay a sure foundation for the athletes to perform well under pressure when it really matters. This long-term strategy of daily exercises thoroughly prepares their muscles for action. And although one might suppose that such an approach applies only to athletes, this process of training embraces generic principles for skill development which work just as well for the muscles of the mind.

The following exercises are suggested in the spirit of this kind of conscious self-development. This presupposes an overall sense of direction for achievement into which some work on your own Colour skills will usefully slot. However, it takes a bit more than a sense of usefulness to motivate anyone to follow exercises from a book. It takes *your* drive and determination to bring the book out to start with – unless, of course, a specific need causes you to refer to it. From time to time when vegetarians come to dine, the cookbook is fished out! Necessity sends people scurrying to their bookshelves or to the public library to get help with specific problems. 'How to' books then come into their own.

What chance is there of your ever using the 'How tos' in this chapter? Unless you are remarkably self-motivated, any initial enthusiasm you might have for developing your Colour skills will probably survive only if you keep getting further stimulus. One way is to get someone else to work with you. Another is to notch up a success or two through putting the Colours to work. In any event, here are some practical suggestions.

1. Work through the questions in Section Two to identify what you want to put some effort into.
2. Select the exercises from Sections 3 to 6 which you think will be useful.

3. Copy them out by hand (your own writing makes it personal to you) into your diary or a notebook. Use coloured pens, drawings and diagrams to make them attractive and clear.

4. Set yourself a schedule for two weeks.

e.g. Date   Time   Name of exercise
     2/3   10.00   Exercise in Awareness
     4/3   20.00   Re-describing
And so on.

5. Review what you've done two or three times during the two weeks. Make a note of when you did what you had planned and when you didn't. Be pleased if you manage half. Jot down your thoughts, feelings and subsequent experiences, arising from the exercises.

6. At the end of the two weeks get together with your friend to discuss and compare your experiences. Make use of this book to answer your questions.

7. Plan another two-week schedule.

Like the proverbial piece of string, how long you continue this routine is as long as you choose. Obviously you will gain more benefits the more you do, up to the point when you exhaust the resources of this book. Then, if you really have found benefit from forming your own self-development programme, you could plan a new schedule using other books, cassettes, videos, people, institutions and so on. A friend of ours set himself a two-year programme which he first planned overall and then broke down into specific chunks with much more detailed plans combining several resources.

What if this proposal for self-development with the Colours seems quite remote to you even now? You may feel resistance or absence of interest in the prospect of making such effort. Perhaps it just does not appeal. These are quite normal responses. Any development of oneself requires the conquest of inner resistance. Self-development is born out of a sacrifice. But forging your own path of learning is far more significant to your development than any 'given' programme of education and training, however good it may be.

If you are hoping for a rather more light-hearted approach to development, there's nothing to stop you pulling out an exercise or two from this chapter and 'playing' with it. Of course, this way you are quite likely to forget to do it altogether, unless you carry the book in your briefcase or handbag or put it by your bedside to dip into from time to time. In our home we have a strategically placed box-file filled with books, articles and magazines which are 'current'. Every time we embark on a train journey we sort through to pick out the texts we feel like reading and working on. Some get read and then either ditched or enthroned in bookcases quite quickly; others remain 'current' for many months because they offer so much scope for repeated study and reflection.

Thomas Hobbes once said: 'Property is that with which a man hath mixed his labour.' We hope that in this sense at least you will make this book truly your own!

Section Two
Getting Going: Self-diagnosis

If you want to be systematic about deciding which Colours and exercises to work with first, you will find a self-diagnosis method helpful.

A QUICK REVIEW OF YOUR THINKING STYLE BY COLOUR

* Do the Hards or do the Softs predominate in your thinking overall?

* Which Colour do you naturally lead with – Hard Blue, Soft Blue, Hard Red, Soft Red, Hard Green or Soft Green?

* What have you recently said or done which

reveals your preference? Think of positive and negative examples.

* Which Colour do you like least of all?
* What have you recently said or done that reveals your lack of this Colour?

WHAT TO DO NEXT?

When you have made a diagnosis of your strong and weak Colours, ask yourself what matters most to you for your development:

* Counter-balancing a predominance of Hard or Soft overall
* Strengthening one particular Colour you lack
* Enriching the Colour you favour most

Maybe all are important to you. Draw from the following sections the exercises that will help to achieve your aims. A variety of exercises is provided to give you a wide choice. Due to the limitations of space they are not comprehensive, but the range is sufficient to ensure that you cover the essential basics in each Colour. With each exercise comes an application for your work. Try it where possible, and think of other applications as well. Essential equipment is a diary in which you can remind yourself to do those exercises which require on-going action.

Section Three
Predominance of Either Hard Modes Or Soft Modes

If your thinking is predominantly Hard or Soft it could be important for you to give time generally to developing the opposite Mode. This may be difficult since the opposite can embody what you find unattractive in other people's thinking styles. So for Hard people, 'soft' may mean 'messy, personal, private, hidden, and inefficient'. For Soft people 'hard' may equate with 'cold, inhuman, mechanistic, rigid and deadening'. Whether you are Hard or Soft, the challenge is to open out your awareness to what the 'other' contributes and to discover what is valuable about it.

EXERCISE IN AWARENESS OF YOUR OPPOSITE MODE

Every time you experience an irritation, an annoyance, a spurt of anger, a fear, or a frustration caused by your reaction to someone else, notice it, even to the extent of jotting it down on the back of an envelope or in your diary, for example, 'Bill upset me at 11.30.' If you have a Soft orientation it is important that you discipline yourself to make a jotting, to keep a simple record of some kind, since doing this is particularly alien to your natural way of thinking.

Then in the peace of your own home look at your notes and ask yourself what caused your reaction. What was Bill doing and saying? Does his behaviour arise from an opposite Mode to yours? Was he being Hard when you were being Soft? And did your Soft ignore his Hard approach?

Now ask the key question: 'What was good about his approach?'

Further questions are:

* 'What was he giving that I might have overlooked because of my orientation?'
* 'What were his motivations?'
* 'What was he trying to do that from his Bias was the right way to go about things?'
* 'What would have happened if I had not been there?'
* 'How else could I have responded?'

You needn't spend long on this, just a minute or two. Writing your thoughts down might help. Then let it rest. The effect of your thoughtfulness will work on without your having to do anything about it. Your awareness will increase of its own accord, so long as you repeatedly look for what is good in situations with other people. If you have a Hard orientation you will find this faith in the development taking place of its own accord difficult to accept, since your thinking style inclines you to want to delineate things in some precise way. So accepting that things can change within you without exactly being clear about how they will change is in itself an exercise in 'Soft'.

This Exercise in Awareness shows a first step on the way towards working better with the opposite Mode. It awakens appreciation of the positive contribution the other Mode makes. But the opposite Mode, like your own, has its drawbacks, especially when it is used inappropriately. There is a skill to be learned for handling it when it is 'overdone'. This is covered in Chapter Nine, where thinking styles are matched to Colour-Maps. These Maps show you how you can guide people's thinking to do a job well.

If you want to work some more with the opposite Modes, pick out one or two of the exercises in each of the following sections on Green, Red and Blue.

Section Four
Green Exercises

The characteristic fertility of the Green mind for ideas has many facets. In Hard Green there is an active lust for variety, for proliferation and profusion. In Soft Green there is a more diffuse affinity for imaging, analogy and for receiving intimations of the unknown. The purpose in all the Green exercises is to create openings for something new, something different from what already exists to be born.

HARD GREEN EXERCISES

1. **Re-describe** This is an exercise which shows that perception is not the same as observation. The method is to adopt many viewpoints from which to look at something so that it is

described differently from each angle. Out of this manipulation of your mind will come new ideas about the thing under observation.

Practise Re-describing:
Choose an ordinary everyday object, ideally one that's easy to handle, like a tie or a shoe. Ask of it:

* What is it for?
* What does it actually do?
* What does it consist of?
* How is it made?
* What else could it conceivably mean?

Each of these questions throws your mind in a different direction and produces a different perspective on the object. New thoughts about it will be forced out through the questions.

Put into practice:
Then try the exercise on less tangible things, such as any of the problems languishing in your in-tray.

2. **Escape** Here the Green thinker uses sleight of mind to dance around the common-place and thus Escape the seriousness of any difficulties which would bog others down. Such a lightness of touch, with its hints of magical, mischievous transformation, makes possible the impossible.

Practise Escaping:
The art is to practise separating Ends from
Means in order to play with the Means –
extravagantly.

Ends: Take a major social or health problem
like unemployment, or cancer, and state a
possible Goal you'd like to see achieved.

Means: Then what Means are available? Don't
stick to what already exists. This is where you
polka into the outrageous, the impish, the
ridiculous, the risky, the dangerous, the stupid,
the paradoxical, the nonsensical and so on.
Look for the *worst* possible way of doing it,
look at how nature does it and look for the most
unexpected way.

Put into practice:
Now tackle an issue closer to your own concerns
and take the same Escape route to find new
ideas. When you've generated many wild ideas
you can try to select one that could be an escape
from tried and trusted methods – and it may be
a more effective method.

3. **Pursue** The role of Pursue is to keep the mind open in case
any step towards Blue should be taken too prematurely. Often
one is satisfied too easily with two or three ideas without looking
further than the end of one's nose. Given two alternatives,
people rush to decide between them without considering there
may still be several other better options. Equally, we can be
beguiled by an attractive proposal and fail to pursue any adverse
consequences that lurk within it.

Practise Pursuing:
Imagine it is Christmas Eve. Time is pressing you to buy your beloved's present. Now don't be satisfied with two or three choices: try to think of 20 possible gifts within your price range. And set a time limit of 3 minutes to generate the 20 ideas.

Not too difficult, was it? Now try it for yourself so that when your mother next asks you what you would like for your birthday, you are ready with plenty of alternatives.

Put into practice:
The next time you are being pressurized into saying 'yes' or 'no', ask what other alternatives are possible. A regular gambit in the politics of organizations is for short deadlines to be fixed on decisions so that a particular outcome can be ensured. An innocent question from you, 'What else is possible?' followed by, 'And what else?', has a sobering effect on anyone who is trying to force your hand.

Comment You will have noticed by now that by character these exercises are very unfinished. Remember this is Green – the exercises stand in their own right with unfinished results. You should glean lots and lots of ideas, and that's that. Green ends there. Red and Blue must take over if the ideas are to be sorted, developed, sifted and turned to good use. Green does not bring ideas to fruition, it just produces them in abundance. So if you find you have garnered some new thoughts as a result of these exercises, you have successfully exercised the Hard Green muscles of your mind.

SOFT GREEN EXERCISES

1. **Symbolize** Now you need to rifle your children's paint boxes, pastels and crayons, for this exercise is done with real colours. While children tell stories and create what they imagine through drawing and painting, most adults – except for the unusual few – abandon artists' materials with primary school. The modern business world organizes itself through numbers and words, driving out the images of the mind. During our teenage years we are educated out of pictures, and in our adult lives we ignore those rich stores of our personal experience and vision which are not immediately accessible to the spoken or written word. The means of accessing them is through images, but images are not often recognized as an acceptable way to communicate with the boss.

Practise Symbolizing:

Open a portfolio for your favourite adverts. Ransack glossy magazines, since coloured adverts are much more attractive than black and white newsprint. Collect them over a period of three months. Try to get a wide variety. (Not just car ads from the Sunday glossies.) Be fussy. Chuck out old ones as your taste refines.

Choose one of the ads you most like and improve it by making your own. Bring in your water-colours, pastels, sugar-paper and Letra-set. Let your imagination lead you.

Have another try at making your own ad, this time with a different product using the collage method – cut out pictures from magazines, link them, create your pictorial image, stick them together.

Put into practice:
Make an advert in pictures to extol your job,
your department, your organization. See what
the pictures tell you. Try it on your most
important relationship and your most difficult.
Why not subject your latest project to the same
kind of exercise? Pictures will give you new
insights on any subject.

2. **Unform** How can you release your mind from its habits?
How can you find a mode of silence for the mind so that it is
open and available for the unexpected, the new and unusual, to
come in?

Practise Unforming:
Take a lump of plasticine, or bread dough, or
wet malleable clay and play with it. Mould it
into soft curved forms. Pull it into elongated
strips. Form it into squares, rectangles, tri-
angles. Pull it apart. Throw it together again.
Roll it, squeeze it, knock it, pummel it, bash it,
throw it into the air, drop it. It is marvellously
adaptable.

Put into practice:
Let your mind be like that.

3. **Intuition** This elusive, half-heard voice which speaks from
within, foretelling, forewarning, foreseeing, is neglected in our
business lives. Have you ever seen or heard of a management
training programme to increase intuition for effective perform-

ance? More's the pity, since it could be a powerful part of your way of managing. Of course, many successful businesses are started on intuition – but that is seen as a gift or talent, not something you can learn, and it gets throttled once the firm passes its pioneering stage.

Practise Intuition:
Record your dreams. Keep pencil and paper at your bedside in readiness. Remind yourself when you go to sleep that you want to remember your dreams. If you wake up in the night with a dream in your mind, make notes. When you wake in the morning make some jottings on your memories.

Record any event where you get a hunch. Did you follow or ignore it? What happened later – were you right?

Do not be concerned if at first there seems to be very little result. This exercise takes time – months and even years. It requires persistence. It's much more fun if both you and your partner do it so you can swop dreams.

Put into practice:
The exercise of remembering the fleeting experiences of your night dreams gradually heightens your sensitivity to the half-thoughts, the delicate, shimmering, intuitive tremors and flashes that pass through your mind during the day.

Comment These exercises in Soft Green help to keep your sanity when you are under stress. Soft Green takes the mind right out of the 'normal' patterns of communication and releases those mental muscles that are stiff from neglect. A real treat when you are mentally exhausted is to settle yourself down where you have a good view of the sky, at whatever time of day or night, and just look at it. The openness of the sky and its extraordinary qualities of light, even in darkness, reflect into the soul, making space for perhaps a single idea.

Section Five
Red Exercises

We have said that Red is the mediator. Truth-seeking Red brings Green and Blue together, so that ideas can become action but standing as it does in middle ground there is a danger that Red may be overlooked and undervalued by both Green and Blue. Green and Blue may recognize one another as the interesting and challenging adversary or collaborator and subordinate Red to a lower status. At the centre Red works quietly for them both and needs their cherishing. It carries a torch for justice (Blue) and is the grounding for vision (Green). We can all benefit from brushing up our Red.

HARD RED EXERCISES

1. **Specify** I suspect we have all purchased a piece of electrical or electronic equipment only to be baffled by the instructions. If only manufacturers employed writers who were better at Specifying accurately for the lay user. With technology multiplying the computing power we have in our homes, and businesses creating greater dependence on systems, we all need better facility to Specify exactly what we want and need from them. Flabby specifying results in sloppy systems. The sloppy office that systemizes onto computer translates sloppiness into the software and thereby magnifies its problems instead of resolving them. (A fascinating account of this is given in Paul Strassman's *Information Payoff*.)

Practise Specifying:
Root around your home or office to find a gobbledegook instruction booklet. Whether or not you understand how to operate the equipment it refers to is neither here nor there.

Set about rewriting the instructions so that a reasonably intelligent seven-year-old could understand. Use drawings and diagrams as well as words.

Find a reasonably intelligent seven-year-old and see what she makes of your masterpiece.

Put into practice:
Take a good look at the briefings you give your staff. How well do you specify what you are aiming for?

How well do you specify your questions for clarification when the boss briefs you?

How much time is lost through misunderstandings that could have been averted if the briefings had been clearer in their details?

2. **Look in/Look out** A danger for Hard Red is its tendency to tunnel vision. Once it starts off on a path, Hard Red likes to trundle on to the end. It is therefore vital to keep the curiously named 'Look in/Look out' well exercised in order to prevent Hard Red from being trapped into this tunnel tendency. What does Look in/Look out do? It ensures that you not only Look in at a system standing on its boundaries, but also Look out to understand it within its surrounding larger system. For instance, a baby's nappy keeps the carpet dry (Look out) and the baby's bottom wet (Look in). Your information cannot be complete unless you do both. Yet Look in/Look out is one of the most ignored and ill-understood of all the thinking muscles.

Practise Looking In/Looking Out:
Collect six homely artefacts, for example, a cup, a lamp, a chair, a book, a pen, a shoe.

Now play the 'baby's nappy game' with each item.

(Take the lamp: the lampshade stops the glare of the naked light-bulb from being an unpleasant nuisance to the eye, yet it also cuts down the light thrown out from the lamp thus requiring a higher wattage bulb to be inserted.)

Put into practice:
When you are collecting information for a project the application of Look in/Look out will cause you to look further than your nose. Completeness of the truth requires you to go beyond the boundaries of what you are investigating. It is always such a feeble excuse to say, 'My terms of reference precluded me from looking beyond.' The terms of reference surely invite you to put any details in context.

Comment All these Red exercises cause you to dive down into detail, to shift bits and pieces around in your mind, and part of the process involves being inundated with 'data' that isn't yet identified and sorted, added up and made complete. There is nearly always a period when you are working in Red that is messy and puts demands on your patience. Hard Red gets its head down and perseveres so as to bring order into chaos. As you gain experience from these exercises it may become obvious that when you adopt a Hard Red mode you actually have to tolerate untidiness and incompleteness en route and not give up until the job is done.

SOFT RED EXERCISES

1. **Observe** This opens all your senses, 'Observe' being used as a synonym for opening and receiving. Typically, we think of five senses. In fact, anyone can readily recognize seven or eight, and the number can be extended even to twelve, as described in Willi Aeppli's book *The Care and Development of the Human Senses*. Whatever the number, all our senses are antennae which connect us to everything. Through their different pathways they illumine the many facets of our relationships with the world and with people. Sensory observation in Soft Red is impartial. The art of achieving that impartiality lies in keeping Blue interpretations and judgements at bay, in order that the fullness of the reality around can be absorbed.

Practise Observing:

Go to your favourite Art Gallery. Sit down in front of one painting for 10 minutes and let your eyes receive it. Notice what happens to your mind when your gaze is directed in this way. Keep your eyes moving round the picture to keep your response alive to it.

Sit in the garden and listen for 10 minutes.

Lie in the summer grass, face down, and breathe in the fragrances.

Pick a flower and describe it to your friend without using the words 'like' or 'dislike'.

Listen to the news without thinking 'I agree' or 'I disagree' or 'I like this' or 'that is bad'.

Give yourself time at some stage to reflect on what you experienced with each exercise. Repeat them.

Put into practice:
Next time you are at a meeting don't agree or disagree, either inwardly (most important) or outwardly. Observe what you observe through all your senses.

Later reflect on the experience. Did you learn more in your silence than you would have expected? Try it again, many times. It takes time to develop this skill and to see how it enhances your effectiveness with other people.

2. **Code** Is there anyone who has not thrilled on first hearing William Walton's *Belshazzar's Feast* or Dylan Thomas' lines: 'Do not go gentle into that good night. / Rage, rage against the dying of the light.' However good a story, it is made or marred by the way you tell it. Truth needs to be told so that it can be heard. It requires different languages for different people, so we have poetry, art, music, drama, mime, dance, advertising. Bald truth belongs to no one but the philistine. And so that we can encompass the richness of our vast universe of knowledge we also have the languages of the many different knowledge disciplines like psychology, philosophy, botany, biochemistry and so on.

Practise Coding:
Take a topical leader column from a newspaper and rewrite it for a teenage magazine, complete with drawings and pictures culled from other sources.

Put into practice:
Rewrite the opening page or two or the latest company report so that a junior office clerk could understand it. How much of it do *you* understand, anyway?

Or have a go at the annual report of your Building Society, or any august body that writes to you officially. Alternatively, pick an item from your professional journal or some such specialist publication.

Comment In these Soft exercises you are exploring aspects of communication which derive from the intention to represent and discover what is true. The success of that intention depends upon both sides of the communication, sender and receiver. So remember, you are as powerful in your support of truth-seeking when you listen as when you speak. Why not try a rather delightful exercise to illustrate the significance of the role of the receiver? Go with a friend to an art gallery and sit together for 10 minutes or so silently in front of a painting. Then, without interruption, listen to each other's account of the painting. See what each of you makes of it.

Section Six
Blue Exercises

Blue thinking is driven by the requirement of relevance for decisions, so unlike those in Green and Red, the exercises here cause the mind's thinking to converge and close towards completion. Blue is shot through with purpose. It strives towards a goal, both in Hard and Soft: in Hard Blue since the rationale for taking action should be watertight, and in Soft Blue since it really *does* matter what people feel about decisions which involve them.

1. **Compare and Contrast** In Hard Blue, the selection of items for comparison has to be done within the terms of a chosen purpose. (In Blue everything is done to achieve a goal.) For example, it is quite possible to compare an elephant with a mouse by listing their respective features and noting the similarities and differences: it all depends on your framework of comparison. Logic simply demands that comparisons made are sound, that is, truly comparable within the context you have prescribed. So elephants are indeed somewhat different from mice in weight, yet the animals become similar when together they are compared with a fish.

Practise Comparing and Contrasting:

1. Select three books randomly from your bookshelves.
2. Write down the name of a friend.
3. Now compare and contrast the books in terms of choosing the one that would be most suitable to give to your friend as a gift.

Of course you can repeat this exercise with any number of books, and any number of friends.

But if you start to compare entirely different items, like a book with a holiday in Miami, you are in danger of transgressing the laws of logic by failing to compare like with like. Comparisons in Hard Blue can only satisfactorily be made between like things. (In Green you can compare anything with absolutely anything else because the rules of logic do not apply. Anyway you would not be trying to choose between them, but rather trying to generate new ideas, so you welcome mixing things that Hard Blue would never contemplate putting together for comparison.)

Put into practice:

Watch out when you are a party to making decisions that phoney comparisons are not drawn between matters which should never be put into the same basket. It's a trick that is often used to make a supposedly sound case. It is spurious logic. A false comparison can appear to put one item into a good light but if it were to be compared with something truly comparable, then it might not shine so brightly. For example, a mouse might legitimately be compared with an elephant as a pet but illegitimately compared with a computer. (Or is a computer a pet too?) How you discern what is legitimate for comparison depends on other Hard Blue faculties called Distinguish and Test.

2. **Distinguish** This refined faculty of mind enables you to decipher the abstract qualities of significance that separate one class of items from another in order to determine how they can legitimately be compared with one another. A plain example can be drawn from our elephant, mouse and computer. Any one of them might be a present for your 10-year-old, but the distinctive quality of 'petness', which arose from the original intention to buy a pet, needs to be defined in terms of these three different items. Is that quality to be found:

- in the ease with which the new present will fit in with the family?
- in the amount of fun it brings?
- in its being alive?
- in its being intelligent?

Only you can decide. Whatever qualities you choose for 'petness' become your distinguishing criteria. If you go for 'aliveness' then either the mouse or the elephant must win. If you go for 'fun', any one of the three might be suitable candidates. 'Ease of fitting in', one suspects, would rule out the elephant except for the most unusual of families.

Forming the distinctions is the first stage, but the nub is determining which in any particular circumstances are the significant distinctions. Which ones matter? Have you missed any? Distinctions don't exist in any absolute sense. They have to be ferreted out of each situation. The patterns in whatever you are dealing with have to be turned over in your mind until you penetrate their complexity to find the nodal points. If you miss something vital then you can miss the crux of a decision. Distinguishing is an art. This side to logic has a certain 'Greenness' about it, for you have to cast about in your mind, turning this way and that, to form and unform patterns of distinguishing features until the ones emerge which are relevant to your problem.

Practise Distinguishing:
1. Collect together 10 items from around the house and array them in front of you.
2. Sort them into categories A and B.
   * What quality links together those in category A?
   * What quality links those in category B?
   * What is the distinguishing feature that embraces A and B, enabling you to perceive the links in A which are different from those in B?

Now, re-sort the items into two different categories, repeating step 2 again. Notice how your mind generates patterns and how you label the patterns after you have seen them.

Suppose items arrayed are: reel of Sellotape, pencil sharpener, pair of scissors, biro, bottle of correction fluid, glue-stick, letter opener, pencil, number stamp, ruler.

Category A: pair of scissors, biro, pencil, glue-stick, letter opener, ruler, all linked by being 'long and thin'.

Category B: bottle of correction fluid, pencil sharpener, reel of Sellotape, number stamp, all linked by being 'short and roundish'.

Two of the distinguishing qualities in this example are clearly size and shape. What others occur to you? And what if you sorted them into different categories?

Put into practice:
Since distinguishing is both a discriminatory and linking faculty of mind, it lies at the core of all work that requires you to identify 'significance'. Significance takes various forms, such as a pattern, a clue, a characteristic, a label, title, property, quality and so on. See if you can recognize in current events any cases where this has been done sloppily. It is quite difficult to be as rigorous about distinguishing as one ought to be.

3. **Test** The best kind of testing is the sort one does for oneself, subjecting one's own ideas, proposals and initiatives to Hard Blue scrutiny. In essence, Test tries to ensure that only what is really solid and sound gets through. Unfortunately Test is frequently experienced as a threatening enemy instead of a friend. Let it be on your side because it seeks to make sure that what is wanted really will work. If an initiative passes a difficult test, there is increased confidence in it. Try the following exercise as a means of making friends with Test.

Practise Testing:
Take a newspaper or journal and select a leader article that appears somewhat contentious. Your aim for this exercise will be to improve the overall strength of the case in the article by putting its various arguments to the Test.

What's under test? Briefly state the case.

It seems to be based upon:

(a)	(b)
Factual Information	Personal Values
How relevant?	How applicable?
How true, accurate?	How good, wise?
What's missing?	Should there be others?
What's superfluous?	

What now needs to be changed and/or added to the case to make it sounder?

Put into practice:
When you are weighing up a case for action, Test should figure in your thinking about it. The questions above are so useful that they should form part of everyone's routine for decision-making. So that you don't forget them:

Copy the questions onto A3 paper, in bold lettering and put them up on the wall of your office.

Or if you have a very mobile job, write them onto a pocket-sized card, in clear letters, so that you can carry them around with you.

A back-of-the-envelope question to use in all circumstances that require Test is 'If this really is so, how do you account for . . . ?'

Comment These exercises have a different character from the Red and Green, don't they? These pin you down. Unlike Hard Red, which requires patience, and Hard Green, which requires profligacy, Hard Blue needs your courage to be willing to be proved wrong. Being pinned down can be intimidating so if you are dishing out Hard Blue to someone else, explain what you are trying to do, that is, make your intentions visible to the other person.

SOFT BLUE EXERCISES

1. **Value** The saying, 'One man's meat is another man's poison' encapsulates the essence of Value. Value represents the emotive, personal and often unconscious influences which everyone brings to bear in their judgements on anything and everything, whether big or small, significant or insignificant, business or pleasure, alone or in company. Senior businessmen have been known to declare that 'personal morality' never enters their board-room decisions. Shame on them for failing to acknowledge what must occur unconsciously and for not making relevant personal likes and dislikes an acknowledged part of directorial responsibility. We will only learn to operate in greater freedom with one another if we make our personal views visible in our decisions.

Each of us must raise to consciousness what motivates and drives us, so that instead of being covertly driven through Soft Blue, we can overtly, in Red, inform others about what is important to us. This real information about values can then become an acknowledged part of decision processes.

> Practise Valuing:
> Think of a large public building that you like.
> Then think of one you dislike.
>
> Write down at least five reasons why you (a) like the one and (b) dislike the other.

Take each of your reasons from (a), one at a time, and ask, 'Why do I like that?'

Then ask of that answer, 'Why is this so?' and then 'Why is this?' and so on – until there is no further you can go because you've reached some 'final' answer in your reasons why. (You may find you can move three or four times with the 'why' question before you come to a stop.)

> Why do I like St Paul's dome?
> Because it is such a beautiful shape.
>
> Why do I like beautiful shapes?
> Because they are pleasing to my eye.
>
> Why are beautiful shapes pleasing?
> Because they stir my soul with happiness.
>
> Why does beauty stir my soul with happiness?
> I don't know, it just does.

'Beauty stirs my soul with happiness' is some kind of final point in a scale of values in this example.

This stopping point will reveal a fundamental part of a value system that operates in your attitudes to many other matters far beyond your taste in architecture.

Now try the same process with your (b) reasons, asking instead, 'Why do I dislike that?' until you reach an end point.

Make a list of your final values and simplify if possible. 'Beauty stirs my soul with happiness' could become just 'Beauty'.

Put into practice:
Note in your diary the names of your values revealed from the exercise.

Choose a business meeting where you will have some scope to consider what values are operating in the group. When it is over, turn up your diary list of values.

* Do you recall any of those values operating during the meeting?
* If not, what other values drove your thinking?
* Can you name them?
* Were you conscious of any of your values operating during the meeting?
* Did they hinder or help your contribution?
* Did they hinder or help the other people there?

2. **Interpret** This is easily confused with the Soft Red mental muscles Observe and Code. Soft Red is intentionally seeking to be truthful, whatever the personal likes or dislikes. Soft Blue interpretation is endeavouring to do something quite different. It is striving to create meaning and to wrest some sense and significance from insufficient information: 'In my opinion . . .', 'As I see it . . .', 'The way it looks to me . . .', 'How I feel about it . . .'. Oddly enough, good actors, musicians and artists of all kinds do not work principally from Soft Blue interpretation, but from Red Observe and Code because Art primarily seeks to portray Truth. Politicians usually operate from Interpret – they colour the Truth with Soft Blue for consumption. People often ask, 'What Colour is a lie? Isn't it Red gone wrong?' No. A lie is Soft Blue – it's an interpretation of Truth, deliberately turned for whatever reason, from Red intention to Soft Blue.

Practise Interpreting:
This is a game to play with family and intimate friends who can stand your being outrageous and who are willing to be outlandish. It can be played in pairs or in a small group.

Someone starts the ball rolling by telling the others about an incident that happened to them. The trick, however, is that they must use a 'made-up' language. It might sound like French or German or Chinese, but it must not use 'real' words from any language. Gestures and facial expressions, emotions and intonations should all be part of the telling. Those listening can ask questions but only in 'make-believe' language as well.

When the story is finished, the listeners must give their accounts of how they interpreted it. They must describe what it meant to them, giving examples from the story-telling to show what sparked their interpretation. The denouement, of course, is the original story told at last in your native tongue. A prize must go to the one who got closest to it, though this must be left to the discretion of the story-teller.

It is also worth reflecting whether your understanding was better when you heard the story told in real or invented language.

Put into practice:
Jumping to conclusions on misinterpreted evidence is a regular feature of office politics. A wise thinker appreciates when interpretation is playing into gossip beyond the reaches of

> justifiable judgement. We must operate Inter-
> pret in order to make sense of incomplete
> information, but we must also be alive to the
> danger of its being stretched beyond wise
> limits. This is good detective work.

Comment A popular 'game' in business is to disguise real motives. Machismo trade and industry thinks it can dispense with feelings because they are to do with the heart. Pushed down in one place they resurface elsewhere: virulently, because of the suppression. Bringing Soft Blue to consciousness involves much wrestling with half-hidden motives. Digging down into yourself or into others is sometimes uncomfortable, too, but it is worth the effort, for when you can work from the heart all thinking and action is creatively enriched.

SUMMARY

The previous sections have spliced out some of the components of your thinking, isolating them and shaking off their cohesive relationships. Such radical surgery interrupts the flow of coherence between the Colours. This will afford you a depth of entry into each Colour for its own sake, but your understanding of the intricate relatedness between the Colours, and their power when they join together, will be rather patchy. When you have done an exercise you may have found yourself asking, 'Where does this lead me?' It is difficult to relate the parts of the Colours shown by the exercises to the sum of the whole of your thinking. Be persistent. Each exercise, with its own quality and speciality, has meaning and value for the development of skilful thinking. After practising each one you must connect it with the others to develop your understanding of their operational usefulness.

An analogy might help to clarify things. Do you recall learning to drive? In slow motion you practised moving the gear lever while the car was stationary. In order to get the feel of manoeuvring, you crunched into first gear and moved gingerly around an open field. You had to learn the highway code in the safety of your own armchair. Your first venture into traffic was nerve-racking, bringing together steering, gear-change, observation of other vehicles and cyclists and conformity to traffic signs. Regular practice in real-life situations co-ordinated all the separate activities into the coherent skill of driving.

In comparison with managing your thinking, driving a car is child's play. Skilful thinking is more comparable to mastering a musical instrument or conducting an orchestra. Excellence in these skills is only achieved through repeated practice, coupled with live performance in front of both critical and appreciative audiences. Taking the musical metaphor a little further, for the harmonious collaboration of your Colours you need the equivalent of a musical score. Just a glimpse of what this is, what we call Colour-mapping, follows in the next chapter.

CHAPTER NINE

Colour-mapping to Manage Tasks Better

Everyone makes plans for what they mean to *do*, but very few plan ahead how they mean to *think*. They might use agenda and other lists of subject matter to focus on but otherwise people tend to rely on operating their minds spontaneously. Planning the process of your thinking is impossible without a language for labelling the various paths your mind can take, and even then you need Maps to give the paths direction and coherence. You already have the Colours to label the paths your thinking naturally takes. Now we will indicate how Maps can show you how you *should* use your mind, to help you plan and control and steer your thinking as you go along. This helps in any situation that concerns you and is difficult enough to demand your best thinking. We call such 'difficult' situations Tasks for short, but we see them as journeys for the mind, requiring Maps of a special, conceptual kind.

Every Task has its own needs: there are ways it must be dealt with if a satisfactory outcome is to emerge. The trouble is, someone facing the Task is driven by his own thinking style, so he may want to use an approach which doesn't meet the Task needs. And worse still, several people attacking the same Task are very likely to bring the energies of many different Colour styles. Usually such conflict is resolved by the use of power or personality or influence, but of course there is no guarantee that the person with the most of these is thinking appropriately for the Task, so he may lead everybody along the wrong track. A prepared Map, which objectively shows the thinking needs of the Task is therefore very useful. Although you cannot pre-plan your thoughts (data) without actually having them, you can plan the direction in which to send your thinking (process), and exercise control when things are straying too far outside the rough frame-work you have chosen.

The idea of programming thinking was by no means new when computers began: think of mathematics, scientific method since Francis Bacon in the seventeenth century, military planning, work study and operations research. Some of the best work done in the past generation to make this acceptable to managers was done by Kepner Tregoe. In fact everyone has some kind of Mapping system in their mind which spurs or guides their thinking, whether consciously or not. For instance, how many people use Kipling's famous 'serving men, who taught me all I knew'? We have actually worked out and developed a whole taxonomy of 'Thinking-Plans' to match all Tasks, but here we are simply inviting you to draw on your own methods and experience. You can recognize the elements of any thinking process by their Colours, and this means that with practice you can build your own thinking chains out of Colours.

Have a go.

As soon as you pan out your thinking for any Task in this way, you will see the problem. Ask yourself: 'What kind of situation is this?'

Once you know this, it answers many other questions, such as:

* What sort of information matters most?
* How do I resolve the conflict between a Green, a Red or a Blue approach?
* How long should I spend at each stage of my Map?
* What's the best order?

There is no single thinking process which will work for all situations. As soon as you get below the headlines to the practical issues, you find that it is useless to approach a Task today in the same way as you dealt with another one yesterday. Useless, that is, unless both Tasks have the same structure and the same needs for 'process' (even though the information itself is different). When this is so, the two apparently different

Tasks can indeed share the same Map. You can actually use the same one for buying as for selling, for example – and imagine what benefits that brings!

The reason for confused or ineffective thinking is usually that the person involved has not recognized the type of Task or what Map to use for it; whenever they could do so, their performance would naturally improve. The problem is extremely complex, but in this chapter we suggest that a big stride can be made just by beginning to recognize the Task you face in terms of Colours, a language you already have a feel for and can identify in your own mental structure. You can use the concept of Mapping on your own to improve how you plan and steer your approach to all manner of issues.

To kick off with, we suggest you recognize a Task and therefore its Map by the goals or results it represents.

* The result of any situation demanding decision-making is that you choose one option and reject all the others.
* The result of any situation demanding planning is that you succeed in achieving your goal by the target date.
* The result of diagnosis is that you find out the information that accounts for what has happened.
* The result of innovation is that you secure the effective launch of some new product or idea into its market-place.

What is not immediately obvious from this list of four situations is that there are considerable differences in the way you should tackle the Tasks, although your first expression of the thinking-goal may not show this. Here are three examples of Tasks.

DECISION-MAKING V. PLANNING

When you think of moving house, it could require you either to make a decision (as in 'Where is the best place to live?') or to develop a plan (as in 'How shall we bring off a successful move before Christmas?'). The former demands that you choose one option only, rejecting all others, while in the latter you commit only to the actual move and keep any options open en route as things change in the month ahead. Your plan may involve anticipating many decisions and mistakes between now and Christmas, whereas the big decision it depends on is a single choice made at one point in time, right or wrong.

CREATIVITY V. INNOVATION

In bringing about the achievement of something new in your organization it might seem there is little difference between the processes of 'creativity' and 'innovation': after all, many people use the words interchangeably. Yet a creative originator nearly always needs someone else to carry his idea through, to innovate it. It is a matter of different Colour mixes. 'Invention' to reach a creative idea needs one combination of Colours and 'innovation' to bring it through to the market-place requires another. Since there is no universally accepted vocabulary for describing the creative process, Colours are very helpful for clarifying what you intend.

You have probably guessed that whilst creativeness must be driven by Green, the innovation process calls for all the Red and Blue you can muster, with only judicious use of Green. In no other strategic activity is it so important to map your thinking. Take the wrong approach here and it's disaster. No wonder all the great businesses in the world are striving hard to crack the problem. See how long a new product takes to reach the market, how many fail ever to get there, how many should never have got there, how much of the price of a new product in a shortening life cycle is due to the cost of its innovation. Innovation and Creativity need different Maps.

FINDING CAUSE V. RESEARCH

Let's take the process of information gathering itself – clearly a Red activity. If your goal is to diagnose the cause of some catastrophe, to find out why things went wrong, your information gathering will be tightly controlled and reduced through the analysis of logic. Yet if you are gathering information for research purposes, you may well require not just a wider field of view but a totally different cast of mind. Whilst both activities can be described in the phrase 'let's find out', the Maps to follow would be strangers to one another.

Now, if you ask yourself what is the driving force Colour of each of these three pairs of Tasks, you might well say Blue for the first pair, Green for the middle pair and Red for the last. So the maps for Decision, Creativity and Diagnosis or for Planning, Innovation and Research are certainly going to be even more different. In fact if you fail to recognize the differences within each pair you may be in deep trouble. These different Tasks demand that you use different configurations of Colours, in different sequences, with a different spread of emphasis or importance between them and with different patterns of interaction between them. In practice, this means that you seek different kinds of information at different levels of detail or abstraction.

Yet having said all of this, the amazing thing is that all thinking Tasks share the same fundamental model for which the basic rule is that you must use all the six Colours to be effective. We will now use this idea to sketch out the core principles of a few of the Maps, so as to show how you can use Colours to manage Tasks better. We must constantly bear in mind the continuous competition between quality, acceptability, and time, as mentioned in Chapter One. There is tension between doing the best possible job, doing what is acceptable to others and doing it in short time or space.

Making and Influencing Choices

At the centre of all that you do is the making of choices. It's hard to think of anything you do more often, perhaps thousands of times in one day, or anything that is more important. You make up your mind, you reach a conclusion, and that is what you will do. The act of choosing is also the act of rejection and sacrifice: once you have decided to cut yourself off from the other options, you pay the price of all the risks and disadvantages of the one you choose. Equally, the choice you make now opens the door to a whole range of possibilities which were not previously available to you. No wonder free will is seen as one of our greatest gifts and our most terrible responsibility!

Unlike developing a plan, making a decision is something anyone can do in a split-second. Even some of the most important decisions we ever make are made fast. Thinking that leads to a decision results in just one thing: it could be to push the button on the first (and last) nuclear war, or to say 'Marry me', or to buy a house at auction or to resign from your job. The result is the conclusion you reached. Its consequences may be something else altogether. Of course, it is because of the consequences that you often take so long to come to a decision. Anyone can make any old decision, but making the *right* one is the issue. So let's use this universal task of decision-making to explore how the Colours can help you do things better.

It is possible to represent the decision-making process as some kind of system, whose three basic elements are dynamically related. Look at Figure 9.1. We have made this system look like a three-dimensional box, for reasons that will become apparent as we explain.

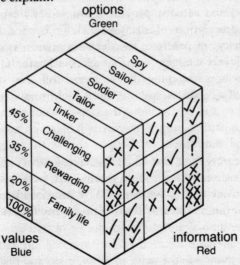

9.1 *Three Colours in choice*

First, the person who is making the decision must have some purpose and objectives in mind (Blue). Second, they need more than one possible way to meet their objectives, otherwise they literally have no options, so there is no choice to make. Third, they need some useful information (Red) about each of the options in terms of all the objectives that matter to the decision-maker. The relationships between these three core elements are interactive, mutually dependent, dynamic. The driving force of each element is clearly Blue, Green or Red. What you value (Soft Blue) drives the kind of options you will generate; you will realize less obvious options only when you engage Hard or Soft Green; and you need Red information about each of these options so that they can be evaluated (Blue) by using your objectives as criteria. The information you need may require both Hard and Soft Red and may be quite dependent upon the quality of its description and communication. The Blue of purpose and objectives is mainly Soft, but the structure of the process as a whole is rational and Hard Blue.

This business of choice is extremely complex, but our purpose here is to show how all the Colours play into one another and actually provide a simple key to the complexity. This description of decision-making is at a high level of simplicity: in practice, the decision process is a hierarchy of many levels of larger or smaller decisions with the three Colours to be seen working together at every level. You will see this for yourself as soon as you use the model for any real decision of your own and try to colour the steps of your train of thought.

Even using Colours roughly will help you avoid the confusion and muddiness of thought that is the usual reaction to complexity. You can be really Green when generating possibilities, really Red when getting the facts, and really Blue when exercising judgement. 'Why decisions turn out wrong', later in this chapter, will make more specific connections with the Colours.

Developing a Plan

As soon as a decision to do something is reached, you must ensure it is acted upon and achieved. If this involves a chain of events through time, or any risks or uncertainty, it's worth developing a plan. In practice, a plan consists of many mini-decisions. It's the way you put these together that makes your plan, for you try to keep your options open as long as possible in case of changes or wrong predictions en route to your goal. Yet you must also take measures that anticipate and protect against things going wrong.

Indeed, a plan always presumes it will change: only the end goal is fixed. 'Whatever will get me there could be a good thing' is a contrast in attitude or approach from the value-driven decision process. Planning is pragmatic and practical, based at first upon realities and facts: 'This has to be done now for that to happen then,' organizing all events and resources into the most efficient network (critical path). This driving force must be Red.

But a straightforward approach can never be enough. You should go into Green even to think up the less obvious actions to take; you must do so to generate possible risks and threats and otherwise unforeseeable scenarios. Just as you will have to use Green to think of ingenious counter-measures.

Planning the future is full of hypothetical and speculative events so you must always judge whether or not the actions that you might take will be worthwhile. Every part of your plan carries a cost as well as the benefits of security, assurance, and confidence. Blue is therefore woven into all your mini-decisions as well as being dominant when it comes to going firm on your chosen route to the goal. Nonetheless, it is clear that the role of the Colours in the whole structure of planning is different from their role in making decisions.

New Achievement

To bring something new into the world and to achieve its successful realization may be one of your highest ambitions. Such success is given to few individuals. Perhaps one reason is that to conceive an original idea is so very different from making it work in practice that the talents required are seldom found in one person.

The extraordinary nature of Green thinking is obviously key to creativity. Indeed one of the most important aspects of the Three Colour Model is the way it places getting ideas alongside the well-established functions of communication and judgement, as a major field of mental activity with equal status. In some people's eyes this gives creativeness legitimacy as a superpower, instead of something curious and idiosyncratic. No longer is it a faculty they associate only with artists and musicians, advertising copywriters and media men, and the odd mad scientist or genius. Through the Colours they can now see creativity as something belonging to themselves.

The other strategic gain from using the Three Colour Model is that you are unlikely to keep your creative effort in an isolated vacuum. You know the dynamic relationships between the roles of the Colours. When you need to envision entirely new scenarios (Green) you need a different set of mind and a different sequence of thought from what's required either for deciding on a course of action (Blue) or for diagnosing afterwards (Red) why your plan failed. If you really want results from the energy invested in painting the future, don't be tied down by the realities of the present (Red) or even worse by judgements from the past (Blue). Both will destroy your chances of reaching any new vision. Remember that what is new must by definition conflict with what is already known, what exists, because otherwise it couldn't be new. And the conflict with judgement may be even worse, because people tend to refer back to long-held and deeply entrenched value systems about what is good and sound. This is why new things rarely conform; rather they arouse dissonance and fear.

The core element of new achievement can be represented in three driving Colours:

Creating the Idea	Development and Communication	Acceptance and Innovation
GREEN	RED	BLUE

Reconciling the opposing energies of Green and Blue is aided by the mediation of Red but also by the separation of each Colour. This increases the vital factor of trust. When someone goes into Green they must trust that they will not suffer from what others will think of them and their unusual ideas. Equally, the originators of ideas should be able to recognize the validity of the judgement that will be made before an idea is accepted and taken up by others. Furthermore anyone with strong Blue tendencies will feel a great need for reassurance when he listens in to some parts of the creative process! Both the originators of ideas and the evaluators of market-place should see it as a common interest that the idea is constructively developed and that information about it is well communicated. Red is therefore a natural ally of both the Green and the Blue phase. Red experience provides raw material for manipulation and extension by Green, whilst Soft Red communication skills convey and exchange information with those whose Blue support for an idea is required.

Innovation, the third stage, is bringing ideas into action. It involves the orchestration of all the activities required to make a plan and get it rolling, overcome all the inertia and resistance, get everyone you need pulling together, negotiate responsively and ultimately carry the day . . . but the day is more likely to be a year. A great deal depends on the successful meshing of the creative effort that produced the new idea and the management of its innovation. To do this well you will be putting together energies of all kinds:

Red for the planning and control of the project and for the vital communication aspect, including a lot of persuasion.

Blue for buying and selling of ideas, the motive force and ultimate judgement.

Just enough **Green** for responsiveness to resistance, and ingenuity in modifications to the original idea.

In contrast to the Creative Phase, Red and Blue now play the dominant roles.

Don't be misled into thinking that all this applies only to massive projects. Innovation is something we all do, continually, on a variety of scales. It doesn't have to be a big deal. Think of day-to-day conversations or meetings you have, when someone comes up with an idea and makes a suggestion. What happens to it? The reflex reaction is to reject it, say it won't work, dismiss it as a waste of time, and so on. It is easy enough to do that to your own idea, even before voicing it. People need to develop a good deal of skill and strength of character to stay with a suggestion and gain it the chance to develop to a stage where it can be evaluated properly.

Managing a Project Plan

Much of the working life of many people is taken up in projects of one form or another. Some projects are your own, and you are responsible for seeing them through; in others you play a supporting role; and most projects are part of larger ones, which can stretch over months or even years.

In Figure 9.2 you see a model that we use for research and development projects, where the end result is often only a conception in the mind's eye, and yet something must be invented and ready for market by some target date. Here is how it works. Suppose you are faced with the task of inventing a new product, let's say a holographic record player. It must be on the market within four years, which is gauged as the time when the public will be ready for such a thing, but competitors won't quite be there yet. First the R & D people need to open up their minds to explore all possible ideas related to the basic product/market concept. They adopt a divergent mental set or attitude,

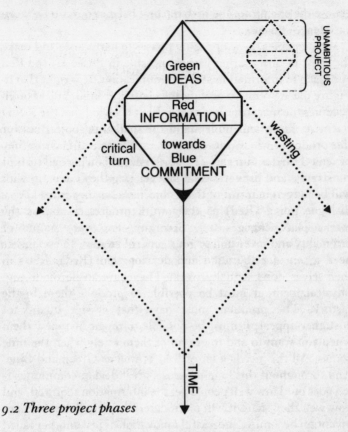

9.2 Three project phases

welcoming all ideas they can generate or borrow from outside.
Phase I is clearly a Green phase.

The successful innovation of a new product requires that
people buy the idea, first inside the company and finally out
there in the market-place. So the final phase is evaluation and
coming to judgement about whatever R & D has come up with.
This Phase III adopts a Blue convergent mental set or attitude,
the polar opposite to the Green first phase. The task of those
who must approve commitment of perhaps millions of pounds
to developing, producing and marketing the holographic record
player is to reject anything that fails to meet objectives and to

choose the one prototype with the best balance or ratio between excellence and cost.

What enables these opposing phases to harmonize and make the most of one another is most notable in Phase II, the Red approach to information and communication. It is right that in Figure 9.2 it seems to occupy the central ground, and it often occupies the most time and space. First it is vital that the R & D scientists know and understand the marketing objectives for this product – which does not even exist because of course they haven't thought it up yet. The objectives will include all sorts of constraints and limitations. Whatever idea they come up with will be judged in terms of these objectives, so they must keep a dialogue going (Red) as their work progresses and as the market-place changes too. Secondly, for every pound of originality and invention to get a germ of an idea, the scientists need a ton of elaboration and development (Red). Ideas in themselves don't actually work. They have to be made into physical form; it must be possible to produce them in the factory. The products must have that elusive quality of customer-appeal; it must be possible to repair or renew them when you want to and to get rid of them safely when the time comes. All this needs a lot of Red as well as Green and Blue. And throughout this long process a great deal of communication goes on. How well people get the information required, and how well they share it will often determine whether a brilliant invention becomes a successful innovation or just another failed product.

Now, for many scientists and researchers, the Green and Red phases of Figure 9.2 are enormous fun. There is no limit to how long they might be willing to reach out for more and more original and stunning concepts. Given a big enough budget, adequate facilities and plenty of computer power, they will go on for years seeking and developing new ideas. So there is a critical turning-point! If you extrapolate the divergent lines until ultimately their ideas are evaluated and a viable design chosen, the investment will have multiplied way beyond the first estimates. Far worse than that, the product may be several years late for the market and competitors will already have mopped up most of the customers with a product that is nearly as good.

On the other hand, some senior executives, who must approve huge investments and are all too conscious of the bottom line of profitability, may well be wary of spending too much time on growing seeds in case the harvest comes too late. Aren't there some short cuts? If less exploration were undertaken it would be quicker to evaluate what the boffins come up with, so the product could be on the market within the year. This stance represents the smallest replica of the diamond model in Figure 9.2 and is simply less ambitious.

A final point to be made about this project model (too simple to call a Map so we simplify even more by calling it the 'diamond') is that of course in any project you would actually go through it not once but many times. The process of development is a continuous 'Out-In, Out-In' with the mind. Imagine trying to do everything in one huge gulp! Moreover, as with eating, you do need both to Open and Close with your thinking, not to mention digesting in between. A crocodile stuck in either the open or closed position would soon starve to death, and so would your mind.

MEETINGS

It is easy to see how difficult it must be to judge how much to invest in developing ideas or products. But we hope you can readily transfer the example to all sorts of projects you undertake, including writing something new and, of course, working in meetings. For it must be obvious that meetings between people will often have an emphasis towards one or other of the three phases, and recognizing their true Colours can help a great deal.

We notice that managers who use Colours as a guide find their meetings much more effective and less time-wasting. The ideas, values and information each person brings to the meeting can be made better use of. The diversity of thinking styles between them becomes much more of an asset than a source of bewilderment or conflict. Even when you are thinking things through on your own, or when others present are not yet familiar with mapping the Colours, it is a great help for effective thinking and getting your act together on the project.

You may feel that the 'diamond' is too simple to guide the complexities of thinking. In fact, you need a simple model because thinking is so very complex that you have to simplify one aspect at a time. For instance, you can hardly ever get away with going through our simple diamond only once. There may be hundreds of feedback loops. The Red information you develop may cause you to return to Green to improve an idea; the evaluation through Blue may require better information; and even the Blue objectives may be modified in the light of opportunities discovered in the Green and Red phases of the process.

Sometimes the process is brought to a halt when something goes wrong, and you have to find out why before you can choose the best solution. The kind of backward-looking, probing, logical analysis required demands an energy quite different from forward-looking research and development information, and this has to be recognized and managed.

Moreover, in any substantial project, a number of other people may be working simultaneously in different parts of the organization, and even outside it. Each meeting or thinking-period devoted to the project could easily go through its own diamond plan. Even in a single meeting individuals taking part usually go off on their own with their thoughts. So the real picture may be a chaotic overlapping of diamonds upon diamonds.

Any phase of a meeting or project must establish the subject and the phase to focus on. Otherwise we all shout at once in a riot of diverse Colours. Listen in to this at your next meeting. You can hear the clashing of energies. This is often seen as a clashing of 'personalities', and some would hasten to muster social skills they have developed to deal with tricky inter-personal issues. You often see someone trying to pour oil on troubled waters, taking the heat out, smoothing things over, not realizing that the root of the conflict is in thinking process rather than social process.

VARIATIONS IN SHAPE

Our diamond model focuses in its vertical axis on calendar time as a key variable. In a period of accelerating change, this can make the difference between success and failure of a project or even a company. Obviously it will be more important in some situations than in others. Secondly, through its horizontal axis, it reflects how much effort is directed outwards in Green, rather presuming that Red and Blue will have to relate themselves to this. How well people operate in each phase is of course important, and so are the numbers of people working simultaneously in any phase. Sometimes you can achieve the equivalent of developing a baby in one month simply by putting nine people onto the job at once.

Strategically, it is possible to observe that people, groups and whole organizations can vary their diamond in both scale and shape when it is related to time. For instance, when a company (or person or group) is habitually reluctant to open their minds wide enough in the Green phase, and takes a long time to reach a conclusion for action, their diamond may be represented as (a) in Figure 9.3.

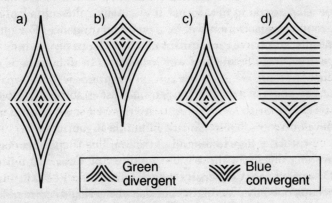

9.3 What shape is your organization?

A company like (a) needs a powerful product position in an unchanging market in order to survive. It will seldom generate new products or methods and will always take a long time to change anything, because it is so cautious in coming to judgement. Its success is due mostly to well-established products and it may seem a tempting target for merger or acquisition. Hanson Trust has swollen to a position of great power by spotting such opportunities.

Type (b) is likely to have about the same number of new product ideas as Type (a) but spends less time over it. However, some of their advantage over (a) is thrown away because they suffer from a long process for coming to judgement. The culture of the company may be very sluggish or suffer from terrible conflicts of interest within, for example between unions and management. Or else they may simply lack a good process for evaluation and decision, putting their trust in endless series of reports and committees. In such a case, management training on an organization-wide basis would be worthwhile, especially if it involved Systems. Two recent examples of an Organization Development approach to training have been the 'Leadership through Quality' programme throughout Xerox, and 'Putting the Customer First' throughout British Airways.

Type (c) is the obverse of Type (b). The company's decision process seems quite efficient, but they take a long time to develop anything new to use it on. Again, the culture of the group or organization will be a powerful influence. For quick results, the active recruitment of a few Green people into key positions may be the best way forward. If head-hunting is not enough, there are just a few consulting groups who are capable of carrying out training programmes for managers and staff, which can bring out the creativity that is not being used and develop a more Green climate within the organization.

Type (d) is here to remind us that our kite-shaped diamonds are showing only the basic opposition of Green and Blue, Divergent and Convergent phases. In truth, Red will often occupy not only a mediating but also a central and commanding position in thinking, especially where many different people are involved. Much communication depends on Red for its quality and effectiveness. Gathering and sharing all the necessary information probably occupies more time than Blue and Green put together. Type (d) simply reflects the company where this important function is out of proportion. Data for data's sake, never mind whether or not it is real information; endless talking-shop meetings; streams of telephone calls and internal memos copied to long distribution lists. This syndrome is the caricature of the Civil Service, with its batteries of forms in triplicate and management by committee. Yet many a virile commercial organization may well fall victim to the seductions of Information Technology. If you have a computer on every desk, use them for everything. If a message is easily sent, send plenty. If the word processor can edit, churn out more drafts. In short, Red data can easily hold centre stage, and must always be aware that its real role is to connect Green idea-striving with Blue judgement through the invincible position of Truth.

The ideal shape for our diamond will be something like Figure 9.4. The reach-out for ideas is with wide open minds and great energy. Evaluation converges swiftly to the point of decision, using information which is adequate over the whole range, without excess or redundancy. The time span between initiation and decision is short. This is how we would like to be, more of the time. What about your organization?

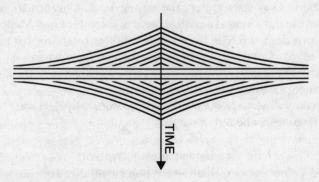

TIME

9.4 The diamond without price

Why Do Decisions Turn Out Wrong?

No one seriously believes that all their decisions are right. A decision made at one time, with all the soundness in the world, is often proved wrong by the events that unfold later. In many cases the information is simply not available anywhere in the world, as when a company is advancing at the leading edge of technology (which is what makes innovation so risky or exciting, depending on your thinking style!). Some of the most able people we know are pleased to feel they get more than 70% of their decisions right – and how do you score that? What concerns us here are decisions that turn out wrong, when afterwards you feel like kicking yourself. How can you raise your batting average?

One way is to be more aware of how you are using your mind when making decisions. Of course, this makes you kick yourself more often than if you were sublimely innocent, but it does raise your score of successes. 'I could have thought better,' is a useful step towards ensuring you don't lose out the next time in the same way.

The approach we want to take here is to assume that no one in their right mind makes a wrong decision on purpose: it's just that they do not handle the available information well enough. Everyone is trying to do the right thing, and do it right. It is the direction in which they send their minds that they get wrong, because they may collect the wrong kind of information or miss the right kind at a critical point in their thinking. Mapping tasks is designed to help by suggesting the questions that must be asked. Colour-mapping is more easily done when you can match the reasons why decisions turn out wrong with the kinds of energy natural to each of the six Colours.

You will already realize that the reasons why decisions turn out wrong can be put down to:

1. Lack of ideas
2. Inadequate information
3. Poor use of judgement

But this is clearly far too general to be helpful. So now we want to show (a) how your thinking energies cause you to send your mind out in six directions, each of which brings in a different kind of 'information' (Figure 9.5), and (b) how the six Colours relate specifically to the reasons why decisions turn out wrong.

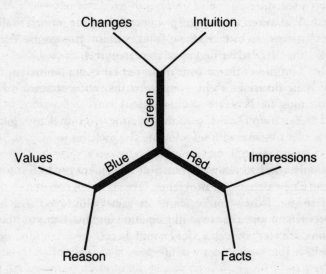

9.5

Lack of ideas Lack of Green Thinking Energies

What you probably failed to do:

* You never even considered the best option.
* You got taken in by and failed to challenge all sorts of assumptions, such as the way things are normally done and the constraints that applied.
* You didn't exercise any ingenuity in the way you saw things.
* You slowed down and stopped developing further options just before you reached the good one.

If only you had switched on more of your Hard Green energy. Then you would consciously have gone out to look for new angles. You would have made much better use of your knowledge and experience by looking around for all the ways you could find to change your perceptions and thus get those new ideas. You could have done all that but still failed to get the winning idea. If so, perhaps it was because:

* You refused to listen to your gut feeling, your intuition, because somehow you felt the need for a bit more hard evidence.
* You weren't able to keep your mind supple enough to allow new ideas to take shape. You couldn't free yourself from the dreaded hardening of the categories.
* You didn't throw your mind out far enough into painting the future in a variety of scenarios, but just stuck on the most likely way it would unfold.
* You didn't use all your imagination; you stuck too close to the obvious without allowing the pictures to form in your mind and tell you something new.

If only you had allowed your Soft Green energy to bring you into a new dimension altogether. This is much more like a kind of magic. When you're alight in this Colour you feel high excitement and a sense of illumination and inspiration. Maybe you didn't let yourself go far enough because you couldn't quite believe that a good idea would come.

Inadequate information Lack of Red Thinking Energies
What you probably failed to do:

* The questions you asked were not specific or accurate enough to provide the information demanded by your objectives.
* You did not untangle all the complexities far enough to recognize in which category a certain piece of information belonged.
* You failed to see either the big picture or the detail.

If only you had put on your Hard Red hat. Then you could actually have enjoyed the discipline required to achieve accuracy and completeness. You would have formulated probing questions and made sure the answers were explicit and quantifiable enough to be verified. In this way you could refine the quality of the information and check out anything that seemed doubtful. You may have felt there was not enough time to do such a thorough job or wanted to avoid being swamped with inessential facts and figures. You may even have done so much of that that you failed to see beyond the hard material. Could you have missed the wood for the trees?

* Did you miss or ignore the more subtle implications of the issue, the music behind the words?
* Were you sensitive enough to all that could have been seen and heard and felt?
* Were you even dealing with the right decision or seeking information which was way beyond or below the level of the real issue?

If only you had put on your Soft Red hat. Then you would have put more energy into listening and noticing, especially reading between the lines of what people were telling you. Further, you'd have been more careful to brief people well about what you really wanted to know. The trouble is, it's so easy to assume that straightforward questions will be plainly understood and will merit straightforward answers that you miss the real message.

Poor judgement Lack of Blue Thinking Energies
What so easily happens is:

* You compare things that really are not comparable in this context. You deviate from straight thinking, unwittingly of course.
* You fail to see what distinguishes things that seem alike but are not, because your criteria were not tight enough. Or else you fail to pick up a significant pattern in your information which proves crucial.
* You too readily fell in with your first thoughts, say, about absolute musts or risks, without subjecting them to critical test.

If only you had turned to your Hard Blue reason. At least you can rely on logical structure to make sure that the way you are thinking is sound so that the decision ought to work. In a Hard Blue mood you are determined that whatever information is available, at least you use it well. Unfortunately, it is easy to be carried away by the power of your emotions and feelings so that in striving for what you want you lose sight of the demands of reason and reality.

The most likely reasons of all for making a wrong decision are to do with:

* A poor set of criteria which does not reflect accurately what really matters or how much each criterion matters.
* Misinterpretation and making wrong connections.
* Making wrong guesses about the future.
* Indecisiveness or even evading the issue.

When you involve your Soft Blue you harness the kind of information that can drive the whole process of making decisions. Recognizing this, you are more likely to invest the effort needed to understand your own values and objectives. However, this understanding requires so much care and skill that no one achieves it every time.

The whole point about choice is that you can get it wrong. We hope to have shown in this chapter that when you make a choice a great deal depends upon the process you use to think it all through. There is choice about the process itself as well, and if you get this wrong there will be consequences.

Some Conclusions

It is amazing how often the giant leaps forward of mankind have been met with utter scorn. Many of the greatest works of art, the finest operas, the most significant breakthroughs in science have almost succumbed to resistance and even outright rejection at first. Indeed, who knows how many valid potential breakthroughs have simply failed to break through.

One of the underlying messages in this book has been the potential for everyone to improve their performance through awareness of their thinking style. This seems to take on greater and greater significance, wherever people are struggling to respond to change, to anticipate change or to bring about some new achievement.

There are clearly implications within this chapter not only for management in general but, in particular, for the directors of organizations large and small. We are thinking especially of the diamond model, the decision box and the contrast between creativity and innovation.

In his recent book *The Learning Organization: the need for directors who think*, Bob Garratt puts his finger on several related issues. One is the organization as a giant 'learning system': the first step in learning could be awareness. Another is the idea of the 'brain of the firm' as the key role of directors and top management, managing the strategic boundaries between functions within the organization and between the organization and the outside world. But he goes on to say that the prime activity throughout the organization is thinking, and that know-how is a strategic resource for survival. He sees the emerging role of a director as orchestral conductor, setting the direction and the pace, reframing perspectives so that new issues can be dealt with on different levels in new ways.

In another vein, the very concept of new achievement may make you think of playing the role of a general, reading all the movements on the battlefield, recognizing the kind of effort or support needed, throwing the weight of the cavalry in at critical turning points. You need to be aware of what is going on everywhere; you need good maps for the salient features of your campaign and to show you where you might get to by following any route too far. Another image is of the captain of a team. Inside your mind you are indeed the captain; you have six kinds of 'player', the Hard and Soft of your Three Colours. It is entirely up to you how you direct them. Which one should you play now, and how will the other five support it? Further, you may be a member of a team of real people striving to bring your project through to fruition. You have to do your bit to help the Colours of everyone concerned to come together effectively on the various aspects of the Task. That is teamwork.

What is your style good for? Where in the innovation process do you get excited and turned on? When do you feel the right to say, 'Now it's my turn: I like doing this bit, and I'm good at it.'

Is it when the task is Green or Blue or Red, Hard or Soft? You might also ask what your style brings out in others and what it depends on others for. We hope that you now have a new recognition and respect for some of the players you might previously have ignored. This applies as much to the imaginary six players inside your own mind as to the people who surround you in real life.

A theme underlying this whole book is that there is something natural in wanting things to get better. It is an assumption, of course. It is, for example, possible to visit locations in dying firms or industries where no one seems to be trying to make things better. Perhaps there is no longer a need for what they do. Or maybe they have done so well that every inch of improvement will now cost more and more tons of effort. In either case, those set-ups have already begun to wither and die. Before this happens to anything you are responsible for, we believe you should be searching for something new.

It should be clear that New Achievement is as much concerned with doing old things better as with doing a better (new) thing, and equally concerned with creative invention and the managing of innovation. What we hope is that for both of these you are now more likely to marshal the right team and face up to the task with the most effective use of your Colours.

CHAPTER TEN

In the Beginning

This may turn out to be rather a personal chapter in places, since it will tell the story, however briefly, of how this work came about, and some of the philosophy which can be seen peeping through here and there in the book. Much of the philosophy is held with equal commitment by both of us, and that's a good thing since we are a husband and wife partnership! But the earlier stages of this work belong to the years before we met and got married, and this will be written from the viewpoint of Jerry Rhodes alone.

Jerry Rhodes writes:

One of our common interests is learning. My career began as a schoolmaster, and when I started my own consultancy practice in 1975 the mission was to help organizations 'learn'. How do you bring about new things for the better, how do you reach new ideas, how could individuals learn to use more creativity and bring it through in their organizations? This was for me the most worthwhile thing I could possibly do, and at once I put all my energies into research on creativity. As a manager, this had been a hobbyhorse for years and now it was to be my livelihood.

'Theory' is not for me a word of scorn, in severe contrast to 'practice'. Organizations which want to learn are surely crazy if they do not make use of all the experience they can get hold of, by finding what distinguishes how people achieve results successfully from what they do when results are disappointing. Yet this is the 'theory' so often decried. All attempts to improve performance, whether by managers in the line, or specialist departments, or by any training function, ought to be based on it. Theory comes from 'good practice' and spreads it further.

There is another side of theory, though, the more speculative or hypothetical aspect, and it may be that blunt men who want to call a spade a spade are prone to react against anything they see as academic. Yet some form of academic approach is often necessary in order to discover and analyse sufficient quantities of Red information. Most companies will not invest in that, and it is even less likely that they will let any of their personnel go far into the Green fields of hypothesis for long enough, because time is money. Back in the 1960s, being responsible for Education and Training in Rank Xerox UK, I was glad to join the Association of Teachers of Management, because it was trying to build a bridge between the academic and the business worlds. I could not possibly have dreamed then that ten years later I would be lucky enough to be deeply involved inside a large business organization on a project that would make most respectable academics blench at its audacity.

Before that project began in 1977, I was to spend some years with a firm of consultants called Kepner Tregoe, who specialized in the rational side of problem-solving in business. Their ideas and work naturally exerted a strong influence on me, first when I was a client in Rank Xerox and then as a Managing Director of Kepner Tregoe. They had found ways of bringing some measure of intellectual rigour and discipline to the messy job of managing the unacademic realities of business. They applied reason to everything as far as possible, whilst recognizing that there really were other factors that human beings bring to bear when making up their minds. Those things, such as emotions and creativity, might not seem to respond to the processes of logic but should be allowed to flourish within a logical framework.

So my approach was to explore how something as wonderful as 'creativeness' could be brought down from its mystical heavens into learnable form. I began looking for the invisible patterns that might be discerned in actions that had resulted in unusual excellence. Not simply in business, marketing and product innovation, but in any fields of human activity where people seemed to have reached exceptional heights: in all of the arts, in sport and war, in love and in learning. It was indeed possible to distinguish certain patterns of thinking that seemed to be common to a wide variety of different forms of endeavour. Then it was a matter of taking these abstract patterns, labelling their components, and converting the results into hypothetical 'rules for being creative'.

Managers generally do not find time for abstract concepts: they prefer practical tools that they can get their fingers around and put to instant use. This has been a powerful motivation for enormous effort invested in making and improving such tools. Only these were to be tools for thinking, not for the hand. This idea led to the design of a whole range of Creative Instruments which embodied in a concrete and practical form the abstract concepts produced from research. This is a process of development which has been sustained over the years, incorporating refinements and improvements as the result of being put into practice by managers in various client organizations. As you might guess, Green owes a lot to this work. On the other side, I learned that single-track concentration on releasing the creative energies of managers in a training programme can cause them re-entry problems when they return to their normal environment. Progress on this obvious difficulty was to be fundamentally assisted by discoveries made in the joint development project in Philips.

The Colours Project

One company heard what I was up to in creativity and asked me over to Eindhoven in The Netherlands. It was Philips. After I had worked with them a bit, they asked me to join a project team they were forming, as their external consultant. The project was to develop a methodology for problem-solving which could be used for improving management performance anywhere in Philips worldwide. Naturally, they were aware of most of the existing methodologies used by other companies round the world but they wanted to go one better if possible, and especially to develop something which would not be too idealistic but would carry the smack of authenticity. In founding my business, I had named it Joint Development Resources. Here was an ideal joint development project with a prestigious organization where we could develop the state of the art with mutual benefit. If we succeeded.

We set to work. There were several members of the team, and we all had other work to do as well, but the prime movers on the Philips side were Dr Hans Horeman and Dr Niek Wijngaards, Hans being in charge. Within four years we had completed the project as such. We had programmes running in several locations and had trained 'Mentors' on site to carry them out. We had a body of learning materials, decently published in-house, including a range of books and booklets, manuals and instruments of various kinds. We had designed what we called the Deva System, Deva being short for a Dutch phrase meaning 'Skilful Thinking'. In the future lay the enormous task of innovation throughout Philips. This is still in early stages, except in the Research and Development function where we have been working steadily over the years.

By virtue of my special agreement with Philips, Joint Development Resources has continued to progress the work of the project in various other companies. Since I joined forces with Sue, we have taken the project through several stages of development, one of which is embodied in this book. Whilst in early years we were too far ahead of the market for the potential of our product to be recognized, in the last few years the market is showing signs of catching up. And we have had more practice in building the bridges back to the main body of accepted wisdom, bridges that the originators of new ideas must always build when they go too far ahead!

What our project team did in those four exciting years from 1977 to 1981 is still, to us at any rate, amazing. (This is a Red statement, not Blue boastfulness!) For we came quite early to invent this new language for thinking, which unites the Person with their Task by describing both in precisely the same terms. For most people, the ability to match the Task with their thinking energy is frequently a real issue. (See Figure 10.1.)

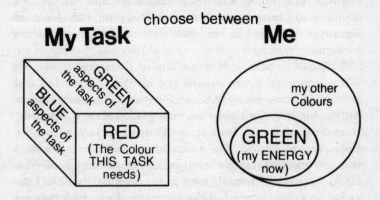

10.1 Making the most of your energy

When you are exceptionally effective, you can usually feel it in a special way. You have bags of go, your timing is impeccable, all that you touch turns to gold, and you encounter sublime lack of resistance, even if it's a difficult task. It is like hitting a six sweet and true into the grandstand, holing in one at golf (I imagine!) or holding an audience in the palm of your hand. Whatever the situation needed, you just happened to be able to meet it. We all know the alternative scene! Figure 10.1 suggests that when you face up to a task, it may demand the kind of thinking energy you don't have much of. If so, you will have great difficulty tackling it well. If you can recognize the task in terms of its Colours, at least you have something on which to build. Then there are several choices you can make. You can look for another aspect of the task that will match your present Colour. Or look for other tasks related to it. Or you can access the appropriate Colour in yourself, and if not, look for someone else to handle the task.

As far as we know, there is not yet any other language in the world which maps the two, one on the other. In concept at least, the language of Colours makes it possible to recognize your situation in your own terms. And since 'your own terms' refers to your mental muscles, you can better choose how to use your mental strength. It is as if the complex or difficult task you face is presented like an exploded machine diagram, with each of its components clearly labelled with the tool you must use and how to use it.

This analogy captures something of the strategic idea we formed quite early on, though it took years for us to bring through all that is involved and implied. The idea was so simple, forming as ideas do in a woolly cloud of the unknowing. It was to produce the basic elements that later formed into the Colours described in this book. These basic elements went through many phases of evolution, taking on various different forms which were actually used in reaching our results. They ended up as the twenty-five thinking intentions which between them accounted for all the significant operations of the mind. We had to find a short word for them, and we gave them the friendly name of 'Thunks'. Here is how they came about.

ORIGINS OF THE COLOURS

In setting down what we hoped would emerge from the project, we naturally pictured how the users could be expected to perform better as a result. How would anyone be able to spot the difference it made? We also pictured what kind of 'product' we would be aiming for. What we agreed on was seen as a kind of toolbox, holding sets of tools suitable for different kinds of management challenge. (Later on, we came to call anything such as a management challenge, a problem, a concern or a difficult situation by the handy little word, 'Task'.) We believed it was possible, or anyway necessary, to identify the kinds of 'Task' widely encountered, and to come up with some form of normative guidance on how each type is best dealt with. This meant adopting or building a taxonomy of Tasks, based on differences in conceptual structure. But it wasn't so clear as this at first.

Looking at the 'typical manager', we decided there was no such person, but that at one level of our thinking we would pretend there was; then we could look separately at various levels and functions that could demand more specific consideration and targeting. Obviously, certain kinds of Task could be particular to the results typically sought in diverse occupations.

All situations were really thinking-tasks; the mind was all one had to deal with them. Find out the functions, find the deep structures of both Task and Mind, and look for elements in common. Then we would be able to marry them together somehow, so that the Person improved their performance on the Task, or the Task got done better by the Person. It could be a matter of mutual understanding and co-operation.

Thus our research had two main prongs: Task and Mind. And it may be worth mentioning that because the project was seated firmly in the conceptual skills section of the Concern Training Services in Philips, our work was given a strong cognitive bias, to avoid reinventing any affective or social wheels. Only later did the results emerge as having strong implications for behaviour, and that anyway whole thinking cannot be simply cognitive.

MAPPING TASKS

In analysing Tasks, we tried to define any one of them in terms of the results it aimed for – the outcome – and this led eventually to the notion of think-goals, thinking agendas and Maps. We observed what seemed to be done when results were successfully achieved, comparing them with what happened when there was a failure. Although our ultimate aim was to find the conceptual structure of thinking tasks, this did not mean restricting our observations to the kind of thing you do in a chair, at a desk or round a table. No, we took any activity as fair game and looked for the conceptual elements in it. There is more thinking in or surrounding a physical activity than meets the eye.

Activities were analysed taking a grass roots approach, trying to pretend no one had ever done this before. What patterns could be found? How could you predict that one way of doing something would turn out better than another? What were the connections and relationships that could be seen to operate? We also looked for patterns in operating procedures and methods that were well established and known to work. What we sought always was *why* they worked. Were there rules and laws as in physics or mathematics? Were there common elements of thinking operation, components that you could use in one situation and transfer the same thinking operation to another?

Wondering how to discover the faculties available in the mind, we struck on the linguistic notion that the language of words is created by people to represent all that matters to them. If there's a word for it, or a phrase in common use, it must matter. Some tribes or cultures develop a rich vocabulary for something they deal with in many complex ways. But they may have only one word, or even no word at all, for something that is of no significance in their culture. Snow for the Eskimo has more meaning than for most of us, and so they have more words for it. Equally a whole new language has built up around skiing and ski-jumping to describe the critical nuances of snow quality. We argued that analysis of words, phrases and slang might lead us to find how people actually use their minds. The components of tasks could have their equivalents in grammar and syntax. If so, perhaps we could find for thinking something like the molecule in chemistry, which you could form into chains and clusters and predict the conceptual outcome of their interaction.

We had great fun, generating words and phrases of all kinds, using intuitive jumps to save time, clustering them and reclustering clusters of similar meaning but widely varied form. We had them in all shapes and sizes, inventing codes of nonsense syllables, batteries of questions, graphic symbols and so on. Gradually we found patterns in the way people behave when speaking or writing which took on a genuine coherence. We had found some basic concepts, as we had hoped. There were, of course, many of them.

Could the results of our work with one hand inform the results of the other? Now began the fascinating process of 'using both hands', finding approximations and even correlations between the components of Task and the basic molecules of

Mind. Looking back, it appears so obvious; but then we were in the middle of it all. What we now understand is much more clear and coherent than it was years ago, because we have used it so often. Then we were struggling joyfully through the mud on our voyage of discovery.

GATHERING THE HARVEST

First we had to simplify and gather in results that would be usable by the manager in the line. We always had commercial goals to meet in our research and development and these proved to be excellent measures for testing the project and being realistic in our approach. This was not a university we were working in, but a business. Each period of time invested, each budget and each year's work had to be justified by Philips' people actually buying the results and earning benefit from using them. They needed tools to help solve problems, tools they could learn to use fairly quickly, tools that could be depended on to work. We came up with a Dual Model, each half capable of operating independently of the other, but with enormous potential synergy between them. Because of the way we had done our work, managers would be able to use these two models on several levels. For Tasks we made a taxonomy of Maps; for People we made the model of Colours.

The first half of our strategy was to build Maps for a limited number of mental tasks that were fundamental and widespread amongst managers of all kinds. Some of them have been illustrated at a simple level in this book. Each Map is a hierarchy of larger or smaller Maps, from something similar to a subroutine right down to conceptual checklists. Each is full of models of models, like Chinese boxes. The user can take hold and use one at any level he needs. In this book, we have not shown Maps in much depth because our purpose was only to show how you could use them to increase what you get from the Colours. Actually, you can use them without the Colours, but we hope you see how the Colours make the process easier and richer.

The Colours were our second, though arguably more fundamental, strategy. We used them first to create the Maps out of little runs and clusters of basic molecules. They were tools to make tools with, very much in line with our philosophy to give managers things they could bend to their own needs. As we used them more and more, we found we could simplify them all, first into a set of 25, then into the Three Colours, and in later years into Six, the Hard and Soft Colours described in this book. Clearly, there are no theoretical limits to the number, but for practical purposes – and this matters to us most of all – the 25 'Thunks', being so much more specific, offer a very wide range of combinations, and are all you need. Should you find the name disconcerting, remember that they reflect thinking-intentions rather than thoughts, and as this is a new concept we had to name them distinctively, and yet retain the connotation. If physicists can have quarks, we can have Thunks! And, of course, they are the invisible energies working away in your mind, whether you know them or not. We plan to reveal more about them properly in a future book.

The first major project with the Thunks and Colours that Sue and I undertook together was at the request of David Steel, then Head of Training at Dunlop and now Head of Human Resources Development at Marconi. David recognized the significance of the Colours for improving managers' perform-ance. Since he made extensive use of inventories to raise the awareness of managers as to how they behave and how their behaviour impacts on their performance, he wanted an inven-tory to help managers see how they think. He commissioned Joint Development Resources to create one. By making use of the Thunks as a specific and thorough basis for the Colours, it was possible to construct a very refined inventory, the Thinking Intentions Profile (TIP). From its early days it proved its value. A number of revisions and several hundreds of managers later, the solid benefits of using it have been proved in several major companies in the UK and also back in Philips. All the data is held on our computer, and analysis such as interfirm comparisons, individual and group profiles, norms for various kinds of work and so on are available to participating companies. (TIP is not used in this book.)

Our philosophy and purpose in Joint Development Resources has been to make our research results available as widely as possible. We in JDR are only few. To this end we are licensing both in-company coaches and independent consultants to use TIP throughout an organization. We provide the training and support necessary for their qualification. We have also found that individuals and members of the general public are just as interested to pursue the implications of their thinking styles. We have no objection to receiving letters from any reader who is sufficiently stimulated to discover more. Our address is 24 Cecil Park, Pinner, HA5 5HH, England.

CONCLUSION

Our invitation for feedback and suggestions as well as further exploration of the Colours is genuine. We are sure to have left out altogether many ideas that are much more significant than some we have put into this book. Moreover, we have certainly noticed the difference between a live audience and an unknown reader when trying to deal with concepts.

One aspect of our dual model of Mind and Task may raise a point with some people, especially as the questionnaires in the book have asked what you *like most*, rather than what you *do best*. In a sense, Maps are more to do with your capability and with ensuring performance on a task, whilst your mental style is more to do with your willingness, your conceptual motivation, and with making the most of your energy. Because of their apparent structure, Maps often seem to constrain and discipline those who follow them, whereas Colours are more useful for interpersonal transactions, accurate listening and sensitivity. Actually, someone who is aware of the Colours operating in them uses Maps better, and won't allow either to lead him by the nose.

What difference does it make when people use these Colours? One thing to hope for is that people are able to give more respect to the Colour they have hitherto played down. This could affect not only their way of looking at other people who use it but also how they use it themselves. This is more than necessary perhaps for Green, which has its special connections with creativeness. The Colour Model could help restore the balance that's been lost through undue pressures of Blue and Red in our civilization. On the other hand, the same could be said for the other Colours in many cases. Just in writing this book, we have both found ourselves growing in regard for Red.

A further change could be wrought by the recognition that Intention is such a vital factor to take account of when making judgements about other people's actions.

But this is a question for the reader to determine. If it is asked in Red, there are more and more people who are using the Colours in their work-place who can answer you. If the question is Blue, then look through some of these chapters again, and you should be able to judge for yourself. But suppose we could take it for Green? In that case, Sue and I both have a vision of everyone in Britain using their Colours before the century is out. The rest of the world may take longer. In politics, we don't hold out much hope: the need for three Colours is too great for it to be recognized in a two-party adversarial system. But for business, we dream of a change in the attitude to ideas and innovation in Britain before it is too late. And for the long term, we dream of what it could do to education when we bring the Colours to all children.

We are really at the beginning . . .

Further Reading

Alexander, F. M. *The Use of the Self*, Re-educational Publications Ltd, 1955.

Berne, E. *Games People Play*, Grove, 1964.

Boisot, M. *Information and Organization*, Fontana, 1987.

de Bono, E. *Lateral Thinking in Management*, McGraw-Hill, 1971.

Bruner, J. *The Conditions of Creative Thinking*, University of Colorado, 1971.

Buzan, A. *Use your Head*, BBC Publications, 1974.

Fabun, D. *Three Roads to Awareness*, Kaiser Aluminium Corp.

Garratt, R. *The Learning Organization: the need for directors who think*, Fontana, 1987.

Guilford, J. *The Nature of Human Intelligence*, McGraw Hill, 1967.

Hochschild, A. R. *The Managed Heart*, University of California Press, 1983.

Hudson, L. *Contrary Imaginations*, Methuen, 1966.

Koestler, A. *The Act of Creation*, Hutchinson, 1964.

Ornstein, R. *The Psychology of Consciousness*, Viking, 1972.

Osborn, A. *Applied Imagination*, NY Scribner, 1957.

Pirsig, R. M. *Zen and the Art of Motorcycle Maintenance*, Bodley Head, 1974.

Polanyi, M. *The Tacit Dimension*, Routledge & Kegan Paul, 1973.

Polya, G. *How to solve it*, Princeton U.P., 1945.

Steiner, R. *The Philosophy of Freedom*, Rudolf Steiner Press, 1964.

Stenhouse, D. *The Evolution of Intelligence*, Allen & Unwin, 1974.

Yates, F. *The Art of Memory*, Penguin, 1970.

Descriptive List of Contents